S0-BIV-392

BETWEEN SILENCE AND LIGHT

720.92
LOB

BETWEEN SILENCE AND LIGHT

Spirit in the Architecture of Louis I. Kahn

John Lobell

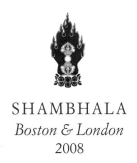

SHAMBHALA
Boston & London
2008

For Mimi who showed me the Spirit in Louis Kahn's architecture

Shambhala Publications, Inc.
Horticultural Hall
300 Massachusetts Avenue
Boston, MA 02115
www.shambhala.com

© 1979 John Lobell
Preface to the 2008 edition © 2008 John Lobell

The author and the publisher gratefully acknowledge permission
to reproduce works in the Louis I. Kahn Collection of the
University of Pennsylvania, Philadelphia, Pennsylvania, as well as
Mrs. Esther Kahn and the estate of Louis I. Kahn for their support and for permission to use the words of Louis I. Kahn.

All rights reserved. No part of this book may be reproduced in
any form or by any means, electronic or mechanical, including
photocopying, recording, or by any information storage and
retrieval system, without permission in writing from the publisher.

9 8 7 6 5 4 3 2 1

Printed in Canada

♾ This edition is printed on acid-free paper that meets the
American National Standards Institute Z39.48 Standard.
Distributed in the United States by Random House, Inc., and in
Canada by Random House of Canada Ltd

The Library of Congress catalogues the previous edition of this
book as follows:
Lobell, John
Between silence and light.
Includes bibliographical references.
1. Kahn, Louis I., 1901–1974. 2. Architecture—
Philosophy. I. Title.
NA737.K32L62   720'.92'4   78-65437
ISBN 978-1-57062-582-4 (1979 edition)
ISBN 978-1-59030-604-8 (2008 edition)

Contents

Preface to the 2008 Edition

It has been gratifying to see, in the twenty-nine years since the original publication of this book, the growing interest in Louis Kahn and his buildings as expressed in exhibitions, conferences, and numerous books, especially Robert McCarter's masterful *Louis I Kahn*. And now, with the film *My Architect: A Son's Journey* by his son, Nathaniel Kahn, we see interest in Kahn growing beyond architecture to a wider public. The depth of Kahn's understandings of the institutions for which he built, as well as the rigor of his architecture, continue to inspire architects throughout the world, and Kahn is now considered, next to Frank Lloyd Wright, one of the two most important American architects.

I am also gratified by the many architects and students who have communicated to me the importance of this book to them, in some cases leading them to undertake the study of architecture. And I am thankful to Shambhala for keeping it in print all of these years. Despite the numerous new books on Kahn, many with excellent color photography, this book remains a touchstone for spirit in architecture.

I must, however, note one disappointment; that there has not been a broader discussion of spirit in architecture over these years. By spirit in architecture I mean a notion that there are realms that transcend our material lives, and that we can have access to these realms through architecture. Kahn expressed this notion in both his words and his buildings. This notion is equally present in the writings and buildings of Frank Lloyd Wright and Mies van der Rohe, as well as other architects and many artists. This spiritual approach is not simply mystical; it is not just a reference to vague feelings, but is highly articulated. Kahn describes precisely the process he goes through, from a realization of human transcendence through various steps in the design of his buildings. This is not just my interpretation; it is what Kahn wrote and how he designed.

So my disappointment is that the aversion to things spiritual in the intellectual culture in general and academia in particular has led to this aspect of Kahn being all but ignored. However, the acceptance of this book by so many shows that this denial is not universal. For that I am grateful.

In rereading my book, I am struck by how satisfied I am with what I wrote twenty-nine years ago. Of course many books have been written on Kahn in the past twenty-nine years, and I have added some of them to the end of the bibliography under the section titled "Additional Resources of Interest." We now know much more about Kahn's life and the sources of his designs, for which I refer the reader especially to *My Architect* and McCarter's book.

I have been teaching a course addressing Kahn all of these years, and I regularly visit his buildings, so I now have deeper insights into how Kahn presents the same philosophy in his buildings as he does in his words, although perhaps with more impact, since buildings have the power to go beyond philosophical understanding to also embody and provide direct experience. A deep examination of Kahn's buildings as presentations of his philosophy is the subject of another book on Kahn that I am now completing.

John Lobell
New York
October 2007

Preface to the 1979 Edition

During my years as a student at the University of Pennsylvania, from 1959 to 1966, I was exposed to Louis Kahn and other faculty who were exploring architecture as an expression of the human place in the world. This exploration took place at all levels: social, economic, aesthetic, and spiritual. Since leaving the University, I have found few others who address architecture with a similar degree of intensity or integration. Architecture is today usually seen either as disconnected formal aesthetic manipulations or as a means for the deterministic manipulation of behavior. In neither case is there a sense of the humanness of the human being nor a sense of the place of architecture in such a humanness.

I have found a fuller sense of human being in some spiritual disciplines, but no sense of the larger social, economic, and cultural contexts in which we live. The way I was taught architecture and the way Louis Kahn practiced it brought architecture into a larger human context and brought a spiritual awareness more concretely into human culture in ways which are rare today. In this book I have tried to present a small part of this view of architecture as seen in Kahn's work.

It seems that, from the beginning of self-awareness, human beings have felt a discomfort with their place in the world, and that culture is a consequence of the struggle to secure that place. This struggle can be expressed in the questions: what is human consciousness, is it different from the rest of existence, and if so, what is the relationship between the two? As will be seen in this book, Kahn addressed these questions in both his words and his buildings.

Section I of this book, "Silence and Light," is a presentation of Kahn's own words illustrated with photographs of his buildings, drawings by Kahn, and photographs of historical architecture that I feel relate to and complement his words. Kahn wrote little, but he gave many lectures over the years. The material presented here comes largely from a lecture he gave at the School of Architecture at Pratt Institute in Brooklyn, New York, in 1973, several months before his death. Kahn's words as spoken are filled with the false starts, digressions, and grammatical errors that naturally occur in speech, but which are awkward in writing. I have edited the material to correct these problems. I have also extensively rearranged the material to place it in what I believe is its natural order, and I have made references to other talks by Kahn. I must therefore take responsibility as Kahn's editor for this material, and can only hope that he would have approved.

Some writers today seek to avoid possible sexist implications of such usage as *mankind* and the masculine pronouns *he, him,* and *his* to refer to both men and women. Louis Kahn had no such concerns in his use of language. Not only did he use *man* and *the architect . . . he,* but he would also say *the architect is the man who,* and *the city is the place where a small boy. . . .* I have tried to avoid changing Kahn's language in my editing. I assume that Kahn's usage in part resulted from a desire to be concrete: *boy* is more concrete than *child, man* is more concrete than *person.* In his work, Kahn collaborated with women as well as men; he had both men and women students; and he addressed his words to both men and women.

Section II, "Architecture as Spirit," contains my thoughts on Kahn's place in architectural history, on Kahn's insights, and on the human place in architecture. Although I attempt to explain some of Kahn's insights, this section should not be seen as a definitive interpretation of his words. I feel that his words must be experienced directly, and that their meaning will be fresh and different for each person. I should also add that Kahn's contributions are immense, and this book is not exhaustive of them.

Section III, "Some of Kahn's Buildings," presents plans, photographs, and brief descriptions of eight of the buildings and projects he designed. I chose examples that represent some of the ideas Kahn spoke about, but the selection is not inclusive or even fully representative. For a more complete presentation of Kahn's work, refer to the books in the bibliography.

Kahn's philosophy is unique in that it exists not only in words but also in buildings and can therefore be experienced directly. There are fine examples of Kahn's work in New England, the Mid-Atlantic, the Southwest, and the Far West. I hope that readers of this book have the opportunity to visit at least one of these buildings. My favorite is the Salk Institute in La Jolla, near San Diego, California.

Section IV, "Appendices," contains a brief biographical sketch of Kahn and of me, notes on the illustrations in the book, and a bibliography.

Introduction

Architecture stands between ourselves and the world. If we define ourselves and the world as measurable, our architecture will be measurable and without Spirit, but if we allow ourselves to be open to the meeting of the measurable and the unmeasurable, our architecture can become a celebration of that meeting and the abode of the Spirit.

Louis Kahn saw architecture as the meeting of the measurable and the unmeasurable. He used the word "Silence" for the unmeasurable, for that which is not yet; and the word "Light" for the measurable, for that which is. Kahn saw architecture as existing at a threshold between Silence and Light, which he called the "Treasury of the Shadow." He felt that a great building begins with a realization in the unmeasurable. Measurable means are then used to build it, and when it is finished, it gives us access back to the original realization in the unmeasurable.

The spirit of creativity, the human spirit, is continually reborn in a person who seeks new realizations, and who thereby carries the burden of enriching the world. In our time, Kahn was such a person, and we are all enriched by his efforts. In making these efforts, he was an exception. He was a form giver in an age that had announced the end of form givers, an artist in an age of methodologists, and a suffering human being in an age of corporate gamesmen. In his efforts to enrich the world, Kahn might be compared with another great American architect, Frank Lloyd Wright. Both Wright and Kahn remade architecture from the beginning, but their personal creative development, which made this remaking possible, was very different. Wright began young with a confidence of personality and a sureness of hand, setting down his basic concerns between the ages of thirty and forty. Kahn was not able to accomplish the same task until he was between the ages of fifty and sixty, after years of creative struggle. The architectural historian Vincent Scully Jr. [5]* describes Wright, whose career started in the late nineteenth century and continued through the mid-twentieth century, as the poet not in words but in form or material of his age, an age he both interpreted and helped to create. Wright said, [7] "Every great architect is—necessarily—a great poet. He must be a great original interpreter of his time, his day, his age." Wright built his buildings in an era of confidence, a time in which a democratic society seemed to flow toward harmony with the evolutionary forces of nature. This flow became the primary element of his architecture. He wrote, [8] "Space. The continual becoming: invisible fountain from which all rhythms flow and to which they must pass. Beyond time or infinity."

One of Wright's last buildings, the Guggenheim Museum in New York (1956-59), was under construction during the same years as Kahn's first building of major importance, the Richards Medical Research Building in Philadelphia (1957-61). Yet much separated the two men, far more than the thirty-two years between their births. (Wright lived from 1869 to 1959; Kahn, from 1901 to 1974.) Wright drew strength from the ideals of Jeffersonian democracy, from such great American poets and writers as Emerson, Thoreau, Melville, and Whitman, and from the spirit of the American Indians who had so recently departed the prairies on which he set his houses joining the earth and the sky. For Kahn, these sources were no longer vital. His was a time of uncertainty and loss of spirit, a time of corporate anonymity and bureaucratic banality. It would have meant little for him to have created an architecture interpreting such a time. So he turned instead to the eternal, to that which transcends the circumstances of any given moment, where he found Order and from which he brought Spirit back into our world.

---

*Numbers in brackets [ ] refer to books in the bibliography.

Kahn was a small man with a shock of thick white hair and thick-lensed glasses. The lower part of his face was scarred from a childhood accident. He was ugly with an intense beauty. Vincent Scully said of him, [29] "Nobody gave off so much light. It was a physical light that came from the activity of his imagination and the aliveness of his intellect through all his pores." Kahn's voice was soft and hoarse. When he spoke, others quieted and strained to listen. His speech was often in poetry and was always a questioning, a pressing deeper into architecture. He was a philosopher-poet as well as an architect. In both his buildings and his poetry, Kahn constantly sought beginnings, which he liked to call "Volume Zero." Taken together, his building and his poetry constitute one of the deepest and most sustained investigations into absolute Being ever undertaken by an individual mind.

Kahn's words are difficult for many. They were difficult for him. Through architecture Kahn experienced a world very different from that comprehended by linear thought, a world in which Order lies beyond the circumstantial, material is light that has spent itself, the human being is the seat of the unmeasurable, intuition stores the journey of our making, and a building has an existence-will before it has a physical presence. The languages of science, psychology, and ordinary experience cannot describe this world, so Kahn felt compelled to invent his own language. It came with great difficulty, and was eventually fit together as though he were working with great blocks of stone, awkwardly selecting each block, polishing it to gem-like hardness, and manipulating it until it fit properly. If he could not find a needed block, he fashioned one, as with "intouchness" or "darkless," words that do not exist but that he needed. Kahn repeated himself again and again, speaking of Order for twenty years, continually refining, finding a tighter fit. Embarrassed at his self-repetition, still he was driven to find a more perfect expression until the whole came together and stood gleaming in the sun like the pyramid: a perfect form, new in that it had never been before, but eternal in that its form was inevitable.

Kahn's words are new because what they say has not been said in just this way before, but eternal because they speak of what has always been spoken of by great poets, each in their own way. These words tell us of the world in which we live and can also serve as an introduction to Kahn's buildings and to architecture as Spirit, something architecture has been and can become again.

Silence and Light: Louis Kahn's Words

All material in nature, the mountains and the streams and the air and we, are made of Light which has been spent, and this crumpled mass called material casts a shadow, and the shadow belongs to Light.

Louis Kahn

Joy

I felt first of all joyous. I felt that which Joy is made of, and I realized that Joy itself must have been the impelling force, that which was there before we were there, and that somehow Joy was in every ingredient of our making. When the world was an ooze without any shape or direction, there must have been this force of Joy that prevailed everywhere and that was reaching out to express. And somehow the word Joy became the most unmeasurable word. It was the essence of creativity, the force of creativity. I realized that if I were a painter about to paint a great catastrophe, I could not put the first stroke on canvas without thinking of Joy in doing it. You cannot make a building unless you are joyously engaged.

I would like to feel that I have not forgotten, nor have you as I speak to you, about the stream of Joy which must be felt. Otherwise, you really don't feel anything. If what I say somehow activates that feeling, I would, of course, be terribly pleased and honored.

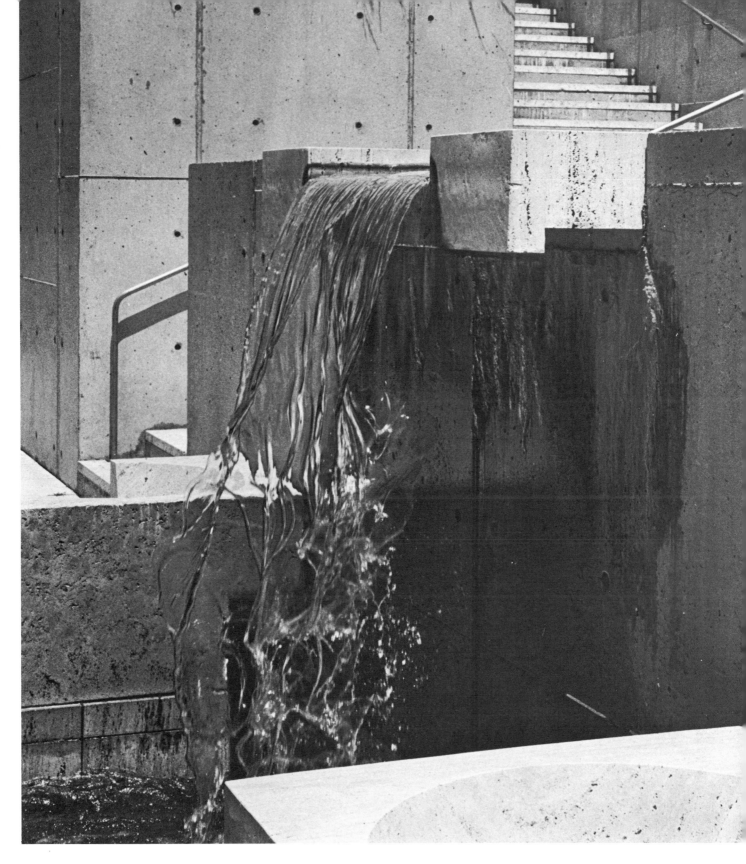

Touch, Sight

I thought then that the first feeling must have been touch. Our whole sense of procreation has to do with touch. From the desire to be beautifully in touch came eyesight. To see was only to touch more accurately. These forces within us are beautiful things that you can still feel even though they come from the most primordial, non-formed kind of existence.

From touch there is a striving to *touch,* not just touch, and from this developed what could be sight. When sight came, the first moment of sight was the realization of beauty. I don't mean beautiful or very beautiful or extremely beautiful. Just simply beauty itself, which is stronger than any of the adjectives you might add to it. It is a total harmony you feel without knowing, without reservation, without criticism, without choice. It is a feeling of total harmony as though you were meeting your maker, the maker being that of nature, because nature is the maker of all that is made. You cannot design anything without nature helping you.

Sight then came about and sight immediately felt the total harmony. Art, which was immediately felt, was the first word, one can say the first line, but I think the first word, the first utterance. It could have been, "Ah," just that. What a powerful word that is. It expresses so much with just a few letters.

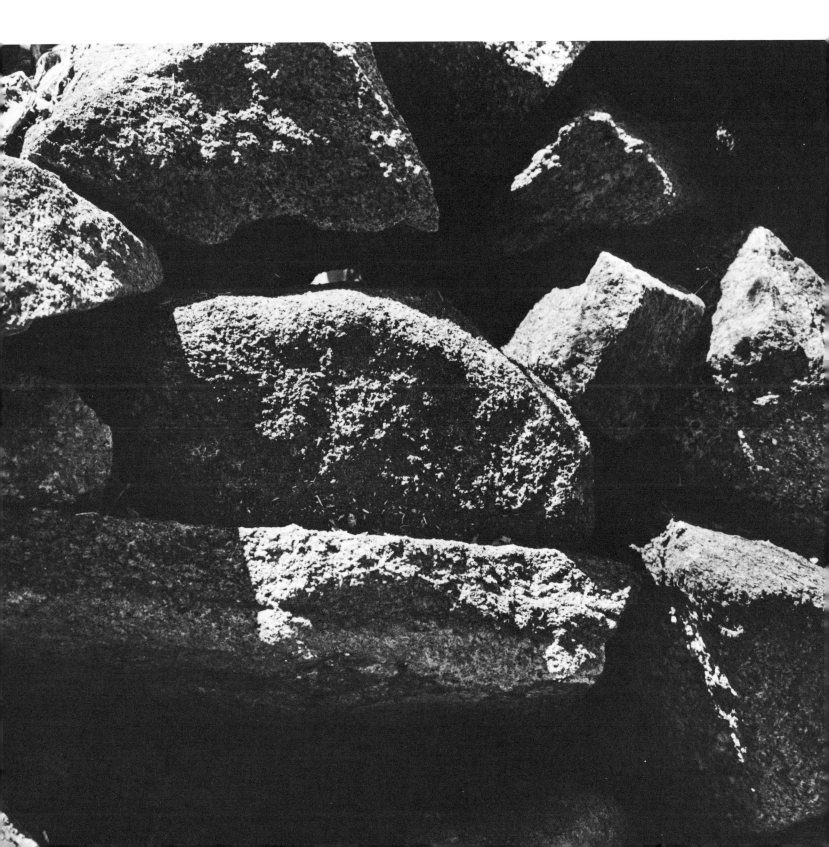

Wonder

From beauty, Wonder. Wonder has nothing to do with knowledge. It is a first response to the intuitive, the intuitive being the odyssey, or the record of the odyssey, of our making through the untold billions of years of making. I don't believe that one thing started at one time and another started at another time. Everything was started in one way at the same time and it was no time either: it just simply was there.

Wonder is the same feeling that the astronauts must have felt when they saw the earth at a great distance. I followed them and I felt what they felt: this great ball in space, pink, or rose, and blue and white. Somehow all the things on it, even the great achievements like, let us say, Paris, a great achievement, or London, all disappeared and became circumstantial works. But the Toccata and Fugue did not disappear, because it was the most unmeasurable and therefore the closest to that which cannot disappear. The more deeply something is engaged in the unmeasurable, the more deeply it has this lasting value. So you cannot deny the Toccata and Fugue. You cannot deny the great works of art because they are born out of the unmeasurable.

I think what you felt was just Wonder, not knowledge or knowing. You felt that knowledge was not as important as your sense of Wonder, which was a great feeling without reservation, without obligation, without accounting for yourself. Wonder is the closest intouchness with your intuitive.

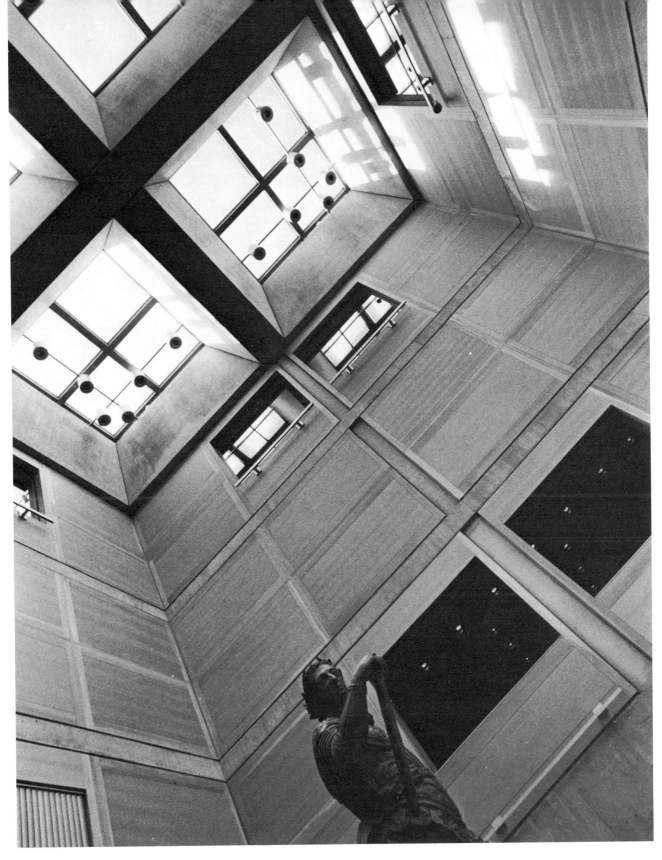

Realization, Intuition

From Wonder must come Realization, because in your making you have gone through every law of nature. It is part of you. In the intuitive are recorded all the great steps of the making in which momentous decisions were made. Your intuition is your most exacting sense, it is your most reliable sense. It is the most personal sense that a singularity has, and intuition, not knowledge, must be considered your greatest gift. Knowledge is valuable because knowing can come from it, and knowing can give you intouchness with your intuition. Knowledge can be imparted, but knowing can never be imparted because it is very singular, very impure. It has to do with you. The life of knowing is very real, but it is personal.

In every thing that nature makes, nature records how it was made. In the rock is a record of how the rock was made. In man is the record of how man was made. When we are conscious of this, we have a sense of the laws of the universe. Some can reconstruct the laws of the universe from knowing just a blade of grass. Others have to learn many, many things before they can sense what is necessary to discover that Order which is the universe.

We must learn to honor the mind of one within whom lodges the spirit. It doesn't lodge in the brain, which is simply a mechanism. So the mind is different from the brain. The mind is the seat of the intuitive and the brain is an instrument which you get potluck from nature; that is why each one is a singularity.
If it is a good instrument, it brings out the spirit within you.

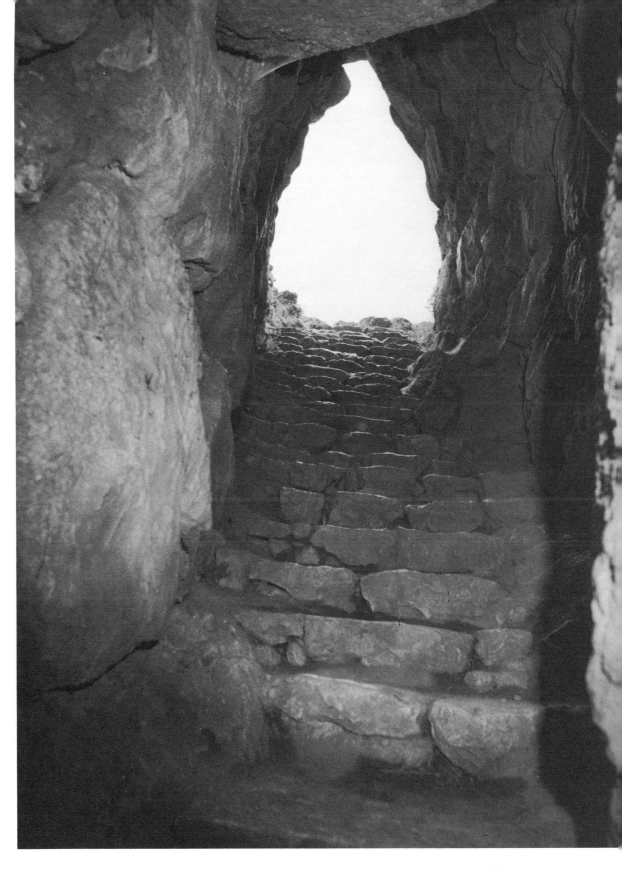

The Unmeasurable and the Measurable

Where is the scientist and where is the poet? The poet is one who starts from the seat of the unmeasurable and travels towards the measurable, but who keeps the force of the unmeasurable within him at all times. As he travels towards the measurable, he almost disdains to write a word. Although he desires not to say anything and still convey his poetry, at the last moment he must succumb to the word after all. But he has traveled a great distance before he uses any of the means, and when he does, it is just a smidgen and it is enough.

The scientist has unmeasurable qualities as a man, but he holds his line and does not travel with the unmeasurable because he is interested in knowing. He is interested in the laws of nature, so he allows nature to come to him, and then he grabs it because he can no longer stand the difficulty of holding back. He receives knowledge in full and works with this, and you call him objective.

But Einstein travels like a poet. He holds to the unmeasurable for a long, long while because he is a fiddle player. He also reaches nature or Light at its very doorstep, because he only needs a smidgen of knowledge from which he can reconstruct the universe. He deals with Order and not with knowing. No piece of knowing, which is always fragmentary, is enough for a person who is truly a visionary like Einstein. He would not accept knowledge unless it belonged to *all* knowledge, and therefore he so easily wrote his beautiful formula of relativity. Thus, he could lead you to a sense of all of Order, which knowledge is really answerable to.

There is nothing about man that is really measurable. He is completely unmeasurable. He is the seat of the unmeasurable, and he employs the measurable to make it possible for him to express something.

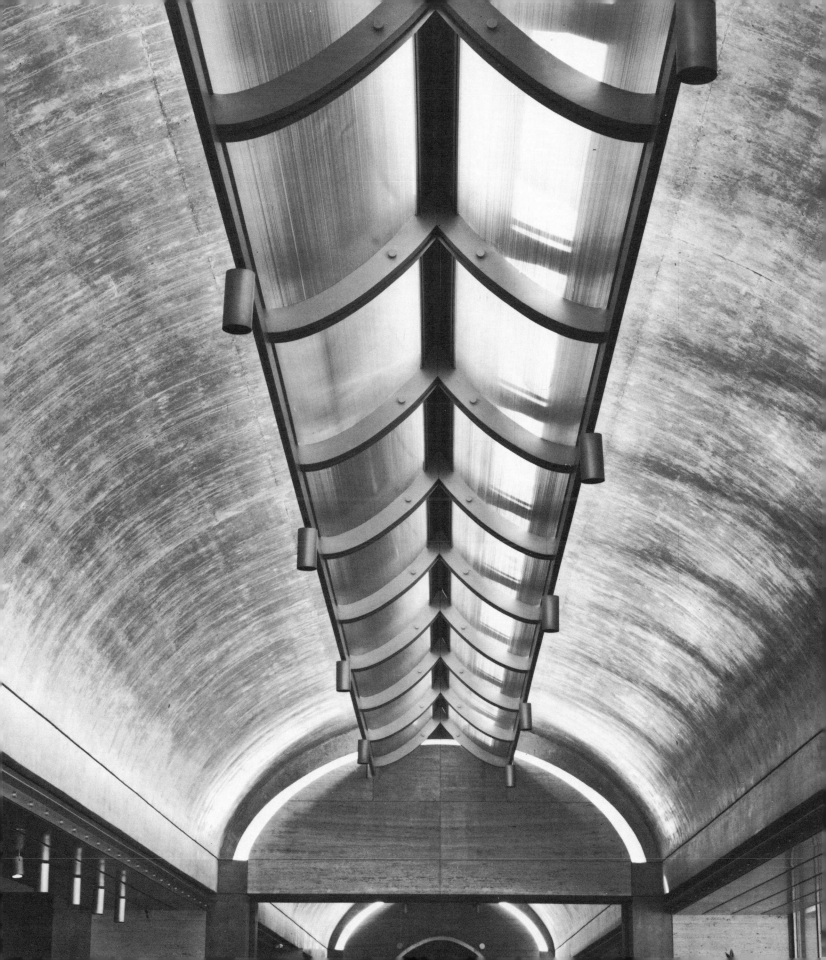

Knowledge

Knowledge does not belong to anything human. Knowledge belongs to that which has to do with nature. It belongs to the universe, but it doesn't belong to eternity, and there is a big difference.

How much can be learned? It is not how much you learn that is important, but how much you honor the position of learning in what you are doing. You must know, to feel your intuition, but you must not trust your knowing as something that can be imparted to someone else. You transfer your knowing into the work you do, and that is your best character.

Everybody is not equally talented. They are all marvelous, yes, but not equal. There is no person without talent. Talent prevails everywhere, but the question is in what way your singularity can blossom, because you cannot learn anything that is not part of yourself. Many of you have learned physics, I am sure, and passed every examination, and you don't know a word of it. That happened to me. I copied the notes of the boy next to me because he could both listen and write. If I listened, I could not write. If I wrote, I did not listen. The teacher might have said to me, "Louis Kahn, it is important you learn physics because you're going to be an architect. But I would rather you don't take notes. Just listen. You will be examined, but I will ask you to draw physics for me." And I would have surprised him. It would be my forte, my way, and therefore it must not be disturbed. If you are crowded with that which does not belong to you, you will forget it; it will never be with you, and you will lose the sense of your worth.

I revere learning because it is a fundamental inspiration. It isn't just something which has to do with duty; it is born into us. The will to learn, the desire to learn, is one of the greatest inspirations. I am not that impressed by education. Learning, yes. Education is something which is always on trial because no system can ever capture the real meaning of learning.

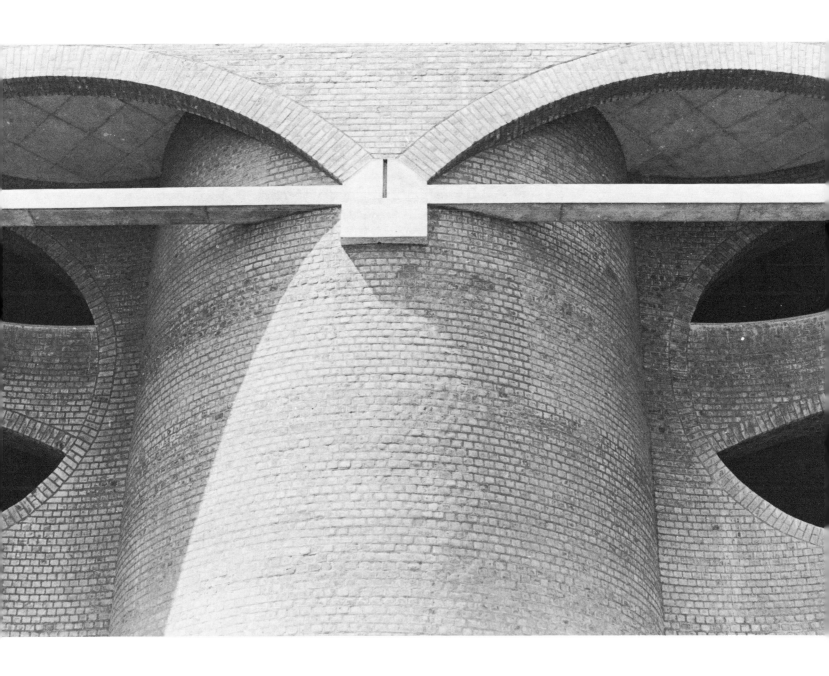

Order

I tried to find what Order is. I was excited about it, and I wrote many, many words of what Order is. Every time I wrote something, I felt it wasn't quite enough. If I had covered, say, two thousand pages with just words of what Order is, I would not be satisfied with this statement. And then I stopped by not saying what it is, just saying, "Order is." And somehow I wasn't sure it was complete until I asked somebody, and the person I asked said, "You must stop right there. It's marvelous; just stop there, saying, 'Order is.'"

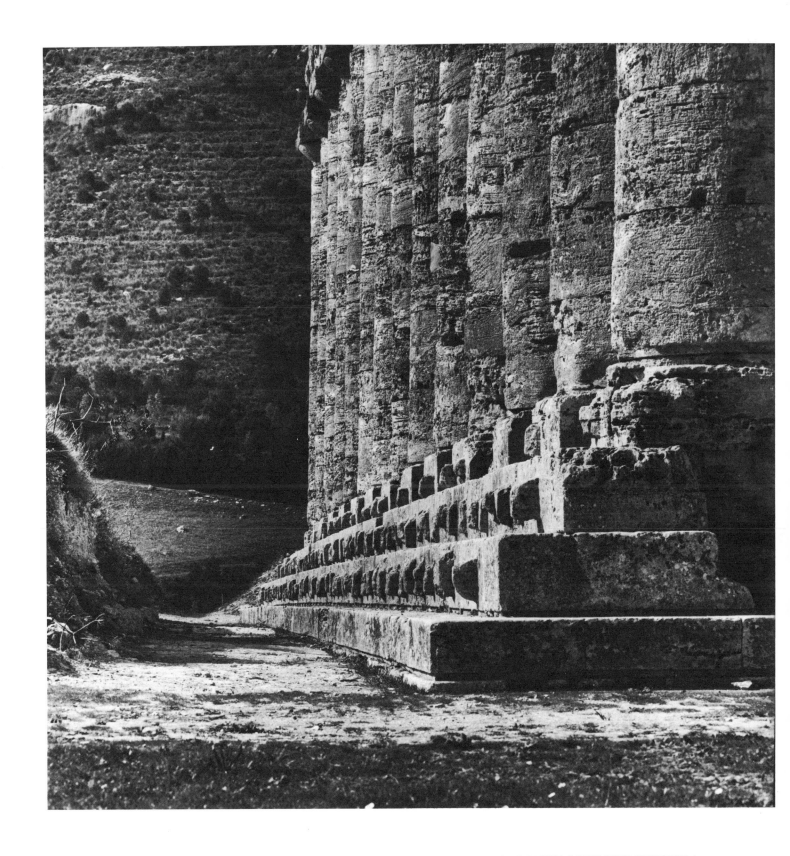

Silence and Light

Inspiration is the feeling of beginning at the threshold where Silence and Light meet. Silence, the unmeasurable, desire to be, desire to express, the source of new need, meets Light, the measurable, giver of all presence, by will, by law, the measure of things already made, at a threshold which is inspiration, the sanctuary of art, the Treasury of Shadow.

The artist offers his work to his art in the sanctuary of all expression, which I like to call the Treasury of the Shadow, lying in that ambiance: Light to Silence, Silence to Light. Light, the giver of presence, casts its shadow, which belongs to Light. What is made belongs to Light and to Desire.

I likened the emergence of Light to a manifestation of two brothers, knowing quite well that there are not two brothers, nor even one. But I saw that one is the embodiment of the desire *to be, to express,* and one (not saying "the other") is *to be, to be.* The latter is nonluminous, and the former, prevailing, is luminous. This prevailing luminous source can be visualized as becoming a wild dance of flame that settles and spends itself into material. Material, I believe, is spent Light.

Silence and Light. Silence is not very, very quiet. It is something that you may say is lightless, darkless. These are all invented words. Darkless—there is no such word. But why not? Lightless; darkless. Desire to be, to express. Some can say this is the ambient soul—if you go back beyond and think of something in which Light and Silence were together, and may be still together, and separate only for the convenience of argument.

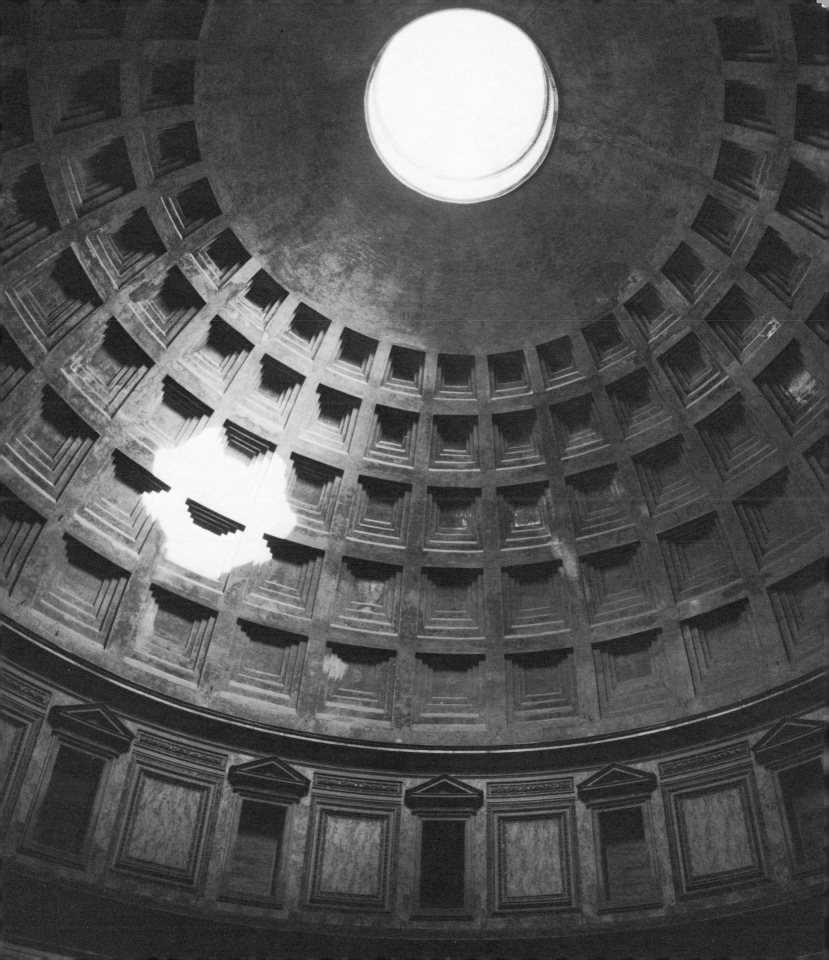

Light

I gave myself an assignment: to draw a picture that demonstrates light. Now if you give yourself such an assignment, the first thing you do is escape somewhere, because it is impossible to do. You say that the white piece of paper is the illustration; what else is there to do? But when I put a stroke of ink on the paper, I realized that the black was where the light was not, and then I could really make a drawing, because I could be discerning as to where the light was not, which was where I put the black. Then the picture became absolutely luminous.

I said that all material in nature, the mountains and the streams and the air and we, are made of Light which has been spent, and this crumpled mass called material casts a shadow, and the shadow belongs to Light.

So Light is really the source of all being. And I said to myself, when the world was an ooze without any kind of shape or direction, the ooze was completely infiltrated with the desire to express, which was a great congealment of Joy, and desire was a solid front to make sight possible.

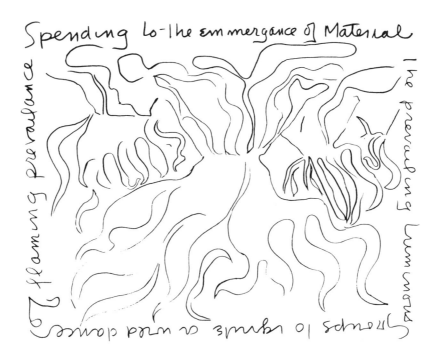

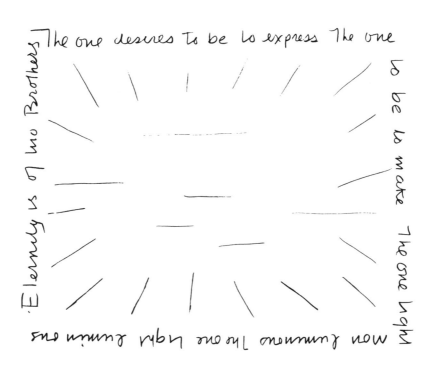

Singularity

Aray of light is not the same ray of light as came before. You are born with nature's approval at a moment that is different from any other moment. Nature gives to everything both measurable and unmeasurable qualities. In the measurable every moment is different, but your spirit is the same.

Nature gives everything to you non-consciously, and you, from nature, get consciousness of the Spirit. Your singularity lies then in just how you are constructed as the custodian of the Spirit. The instrument that senses this is the brain, and that you get potluck from nature.

Singularity is in the movement from Silence, which is the seat of the unmeasurable and the desire to be, to express, moving towards the means to express, which is material made of Light. Light comes to you because actually it is not divided; it is simply that which desires to be manifest, coming together with that which has become manifest. That movement meets at a point which may be called your singularity.

There are as many meetings as there are people. And there must be, in a way, as many meetings as there are leaves on a tree, for I believe that sense must be in a tree or a microbe equally as much as it is in every other living creature.

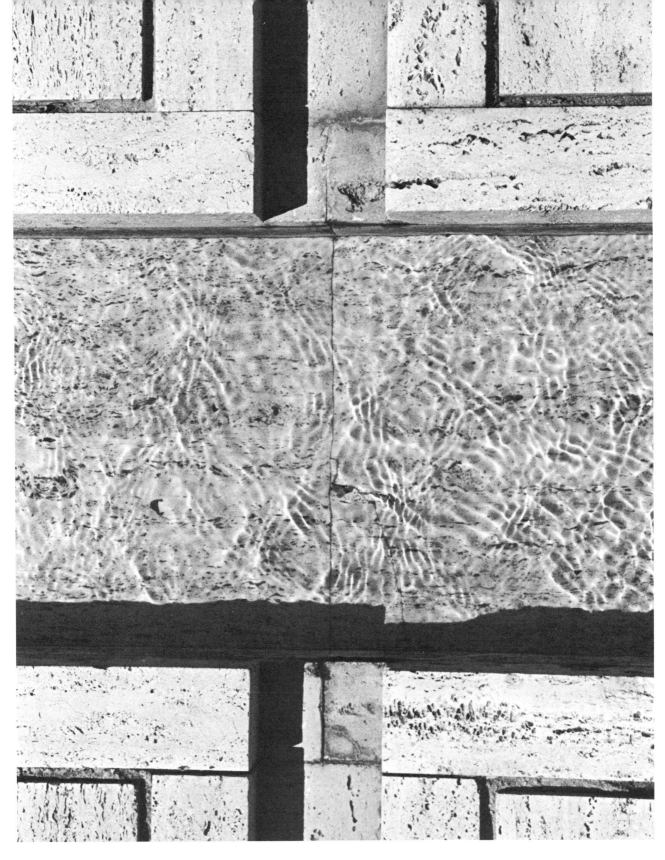

Making Something

There is a distinction between nature's laws and our rules. We work by rules, but we employ nature's laws to make something. The rule is made to be changed, but nature cannot change its laws. If it did, there would be no Order whatsoever. There would be what we think is chaos. The laws of nature tell us that the color, the weight, the position of the pebble on the beach are undeniable. The pebble is placed there non-consciously by the interplay of the laws of nature. A rule is a conscious act needing circumstances to prove its validity or its need for change.

Any rule you have is really there on trial. The greatest moment of a rule is change: when that rule comes to a higher level of realization, that leads to a new rule. To discover a new rule is to discover a new avenue of expression.

That is why dealing with aesthetics, which are the rules of art, is very dangerous. I would say that one should not employ any aesthetics. Aesthetics are realized out of the singularity of a making in which someone, sensitive to how the rules might be employed, makes an aesthetic principle. Aesthetics come after you make something, not before. You can leave aesthetics to someone else, to the architectural critic, for instance.

Now what I have said is a categorical statement, which should be forgotten, because there are those who look at it very seriously another way. But let them think of it that way. I think of it this way because I can work this way and others can work their way. Therein lies the beauty of people, within whom the greatest completeness of an odyssey of their making exists, beautiful in so many ways.

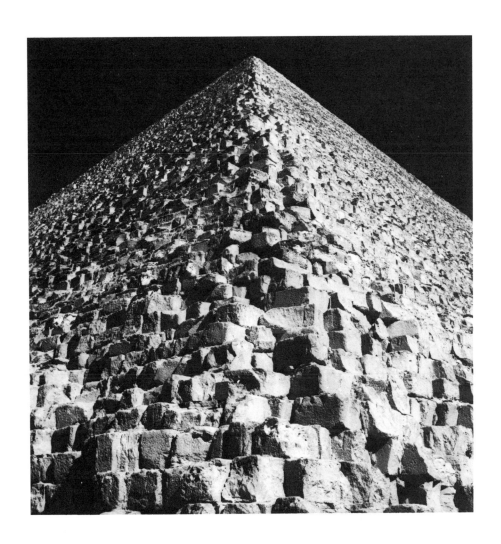

Form and Design

With the sense of Wonder comes Realization. Realization is born out of the intuitive. Something must be just so, and it has a definite existence though you cannot see it. You strive because that existence makes you think of what you want to express. In this drive to express, you make a distinction between existence and presence. When you give something presence, you have to consult nature, and that is where Design begins.

Form encompasses a harmony of systems, a sense of Order, and that which distinguishes one existence from another. Form is the realization of a nature, made up of inseparable elements. Form has no shape or dimension. It is completely inaudible, unseeable. It has no presence; its existence is in the mind. You turn to nature to make it actually present. Form precedes Design. Form is "what." Design is "how." Form is impersonal; Design belongs to the designer.

Design gives the elements their shape, taking them from their existence in the mind to their tangible presence. Design is a circumstantial act. In architecture, it characterizes a harmony of spaces good for a certain activity.

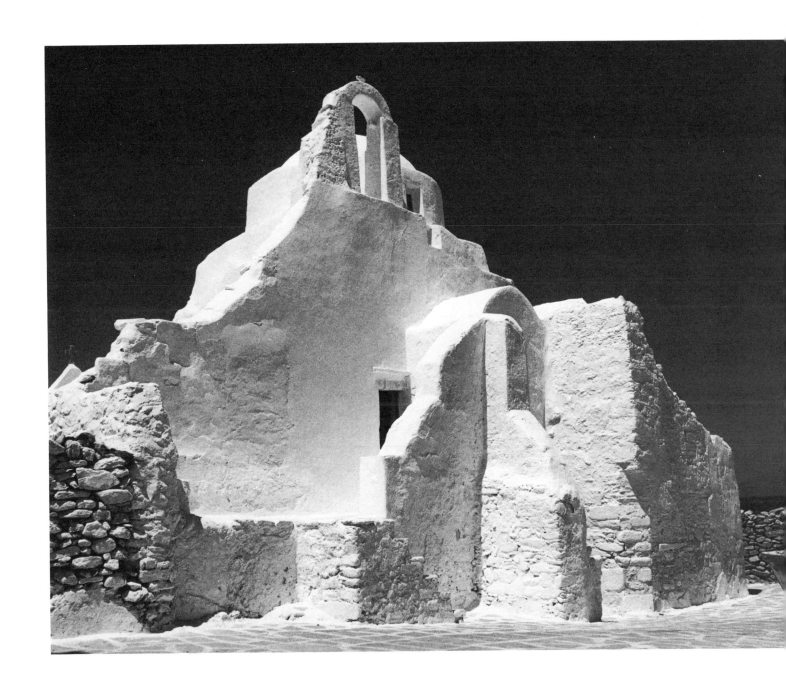

Place

It is a decision coming from commonality that you choose a place out of all places to build, a place where others can also settle. It is a very important decision, of the same importance as the positioning of a Greek temple amongst the hills. Of all the hills, this hill is chosen for the temple, and then all the other hills beckon to it as if bowing to this decision. You do not see the hills now except as respecting the decision of the placing of this eulogizing building, which is remarkable in that it has never been there before.

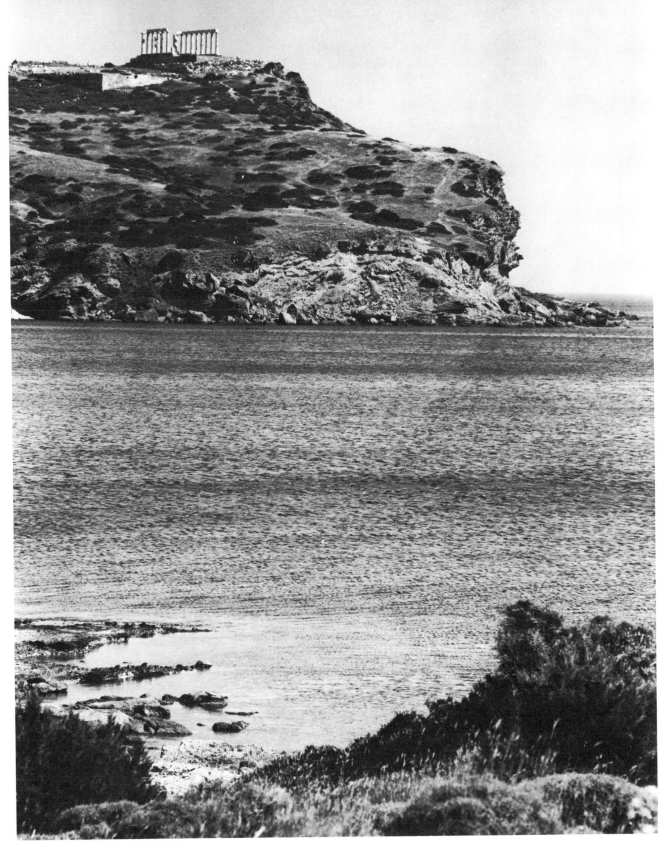

Space

Space has tonality, and I imagine myself composing a space lofty, vaulted, or under a dome, attributing to it a sound character alternating with the tones of space, narrow and high, with graduating silver, light to darkness.

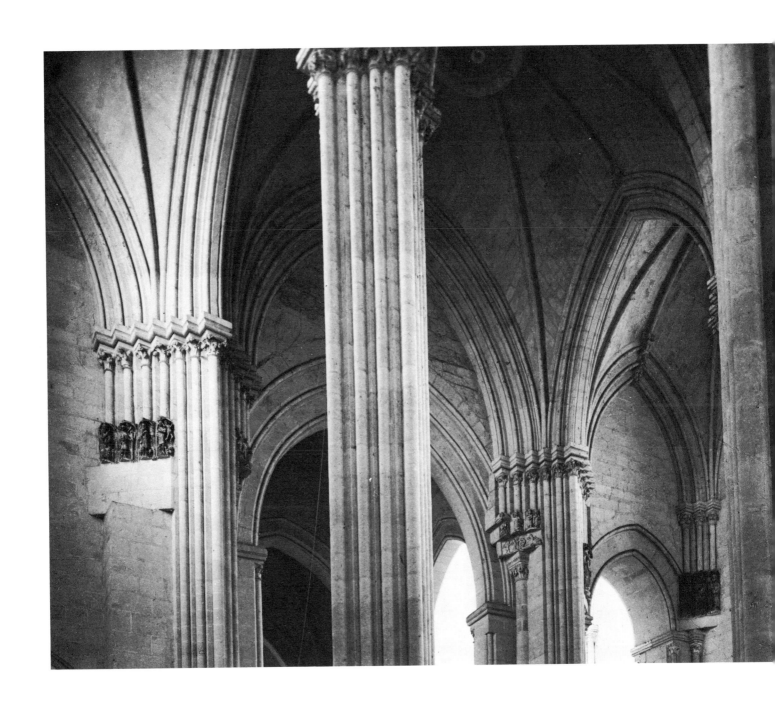

Structure

Structure is the giver of light. When I choose an order of structure that calls for column alongside of column, it presents a rhythm of no light, light, no light, light, no light, light. A vault, a dome, is also a choice of a character of light.

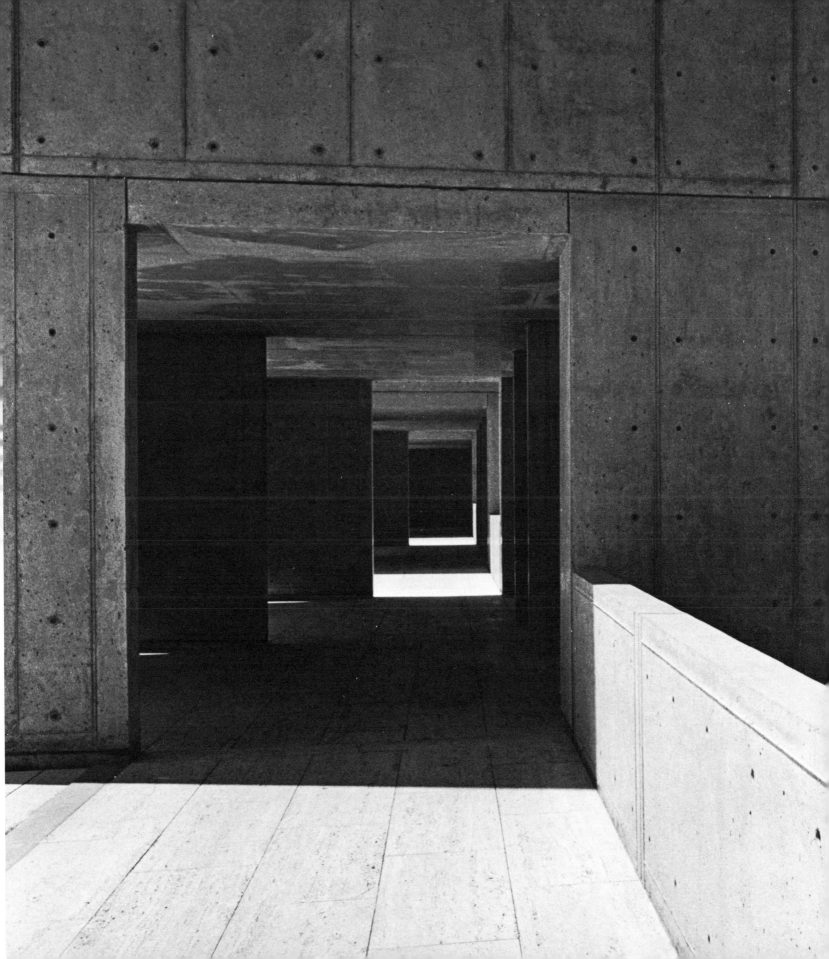

The Plan

I think that a plan is a society of rooms. A real plan is one in which rooms have spoken to each other. When you see a plan, you can say that it is the structure of the spaces in their light.

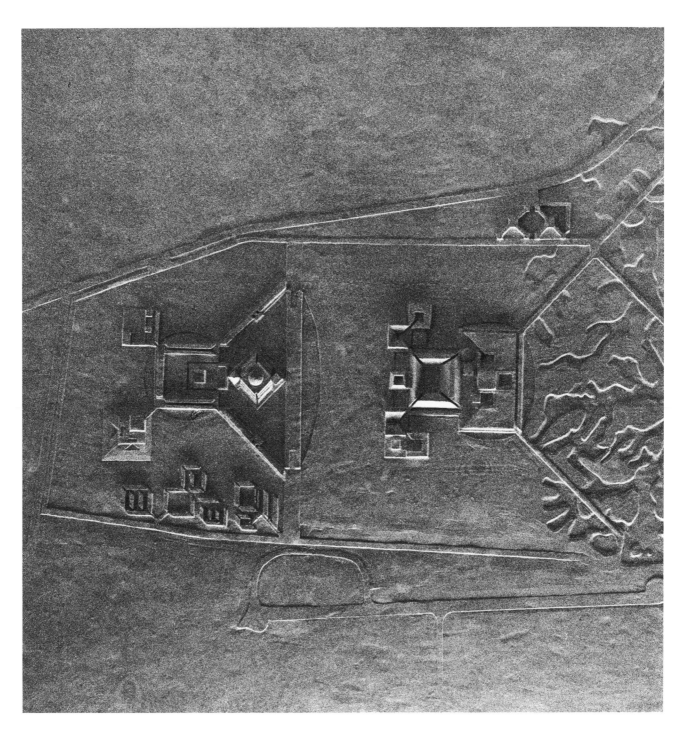

The Garden and the Room

In doing a memorial I started with a room and a garden. That was all I had. Why did I choose a room and a garden as a point of departure? Because the garden is a personal gathering of nature, and the room is the beginning of architecture.

The garden has to do with nature as it applies to a place that has been chosen by man and is developed for man's use in a certain way. The architect becomes the advocate of nature, and makes everything in the deepest respect for nature. He does this by not imitating it at all, and not allowing himself to think that he is a designer—if he imitates how, let us say, the bird plants the tree. But he must plant the tree as man, a choosing, conscious individual.

The room is not only the beginning of architecture: it is an extension of self. If you think about it, you realize that you don't say the same thing in a small room that you say in a large room. If I were to speak in a great hall, I would have to pick one person who smiles at me in order to be able to speak at all.

The large room and the small room, the tall room and the low room, the room with the fireplace and the room without, all become great events in your mind. You begin to think, not what are the requirements, but rather what are the elements of architecture that you can employ to make an environment in which it is good to learn, good to live, or good to work.

Also marvelous in a room is the light that comes through the windows of that room and that belongs to the room. The sun does not realize how wonderful it is until after a room is made. A man's creation, the making of a room, is nothing short of a miracle. Just think, that a man can claim a slice of the sun.

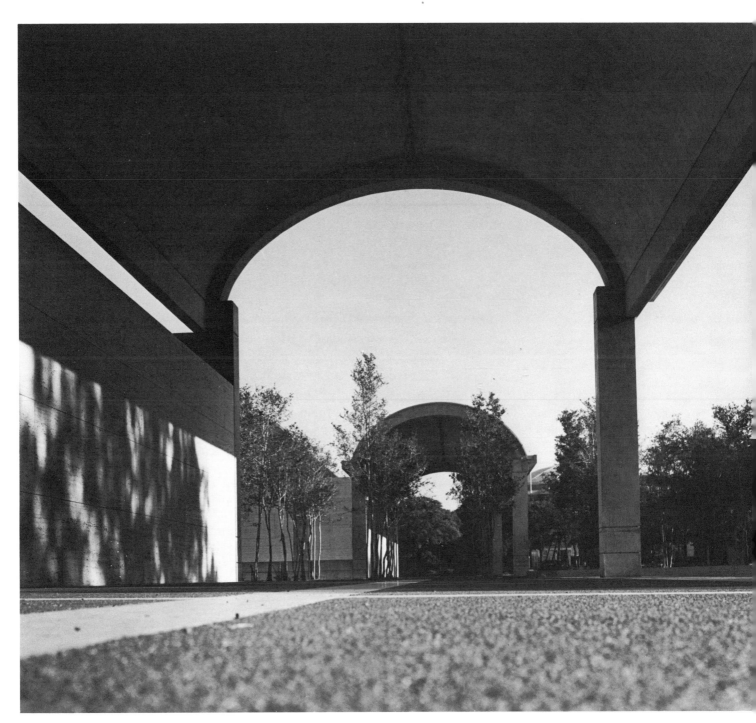

Materials

Realization is Realization in Form, which means a nature. You realize that something has a certain nature. A school has a certain nature, and in making a school the consultation and approval of nature are absolutely necessary. In such a consultation you can discover the Order of water, the Order of wind, the Order of light, the Order of certain materials. If you think of brick, and you're consulting the Orders, you consider the nature of brick. You say to brick, "What do you want, brick?" Brick says to you, "I like an arch." If you say to brick, "Arches are expensive, and I can use a concrete lintel over an opening. What do you think of that, brick?" Brick says, "I like an arch."

It is important that you honor the material you use. You don't bandy it about as though to say, "Well, we have a lot of material, we can do it one way, we can do it another way." It's not true. You must honor and glorify the brick instead of short-changing it and giving it an inferior job to do in which it loses its character, as, for example, when you use it as infill material, which I have done and you have done. Using brick so makes it feel as though it is a servant, and brick is a beautiful material. It has done beautiful work in many places and still does. Brick is a completely live material in areas that occupy three quarters of the world, where it is the only logical material to use. Concrete is a highly sophisticated material, not so available as you think.

You can have the same conversation with concrete, with paper or papier-mâché, or with plastic, or marble, or any material. The beauty of what you create comes if you honor the material for what it really is. Never use it in a subsidiary way so as to make the material wait for the next person to come along and honor its character.

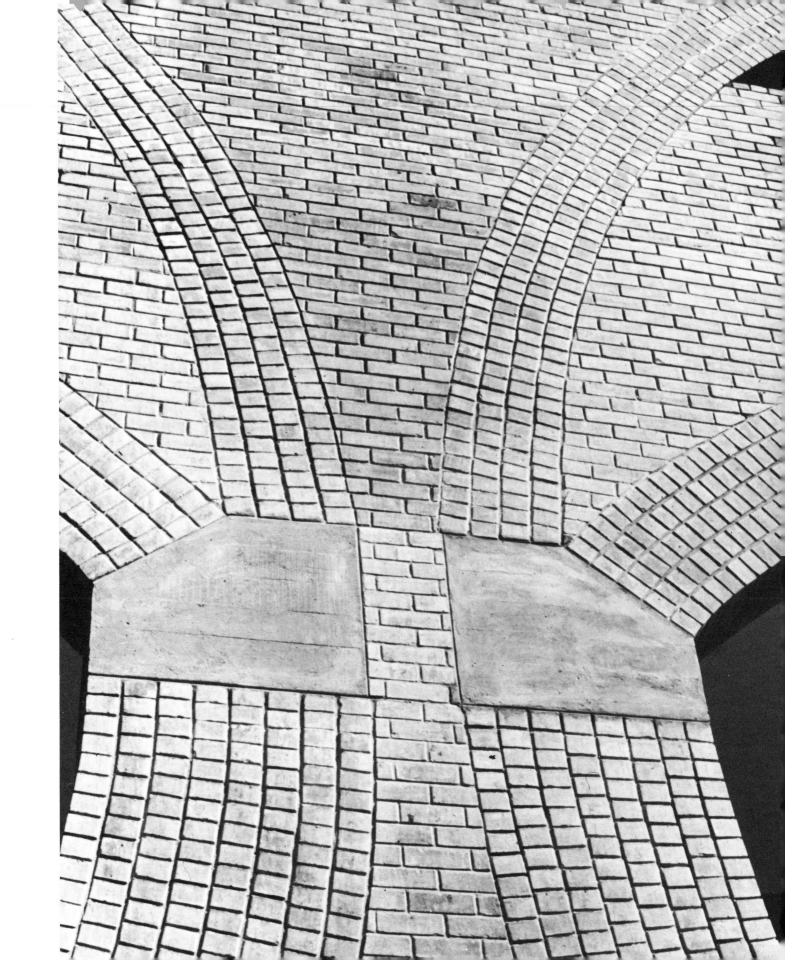

The Wall, the Column

The wall did well for man. In its thickness and its strength, it protected man against destruction. But soon, the will to look out made man make a hole in the wall, and the wall was pained, and said, "What are you doing to me? I protected you; I made you feel secure—and now you put a hole through me!" And man said, "But I see wonderful things, and I want to look out." And the wall felt very sad.

Later man didn't just hack a hole through the wall, but made a discerning opening, one trimmed with fine stone, and he put a lintel over the opening. And soon the wall felt pretty well.

Consider also the momentous event in architecture when the wall parted and the column became.

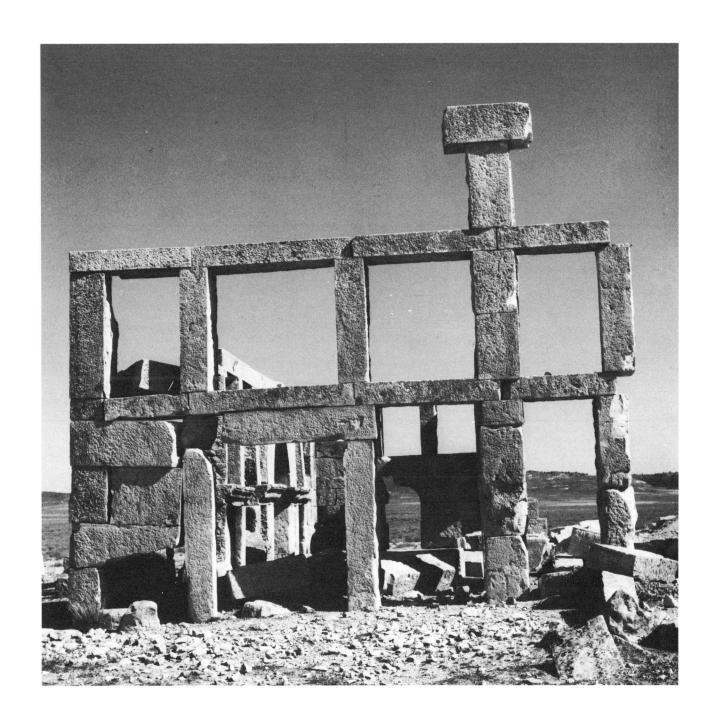

Institutions

Institution stems from the inspiration to live. This inspiration remains meekly expressed in our institutions today. The three great inspirations are the inspiration to learn, the inspiration to meet, and the inspiration for well-being. They all serve, really, the *will to be, to express*. This is, you might say, the reason for living. All the institutions of man, whether they serve man's interest in medicine, or chemistry, or mechanics, or architecture, are all ultimately answerable to this desire in man to find out what forces caused him to be, and what means made it possible for him to be.

Today, shadows are black. But really, there is no such thing as white light, black shadow. I was brought up when light was yellow and shadow was blue. White light is a way of saying that even the sun is on trial, and certainly, all of our institutions are on trial.

I believe this is so because institutions have lost the inspirations of their beginnings. The constant play of circumstances, from moment to moment unpredictable, distort the inspired beginnings of natural agreement. The institution will die when its inspirations are no longer felt, and it operates as a matter of course. Human agreement, however, once it presents itself as a Realization, is indestructible.

The City

The city is the place of availabilities. It is the place where a small boy, as he walks through it, may see something that will tell him what he wants to do his whole life.

A plan is a society of rooms. The plan of a city is no more complex than the plan of a house, not at all. You must realize that it isn't a bag of tricks or a collection of systems, but that it must be true to its nature. Before the institution, was the natural agreement, the sense of commonality. The city, from a simple settlement, became the place of assembled institutions. The measure of its greatness as a place to live must come from the character of its institutions, sanctioned by their sensitivity to desire for new agreement, not by need, because need comes from what already is. Desire is the thing not made, the roots of the will to live. It is the mind of the architect that is best suited to bring all of the forces that make a city into a symphonic character.

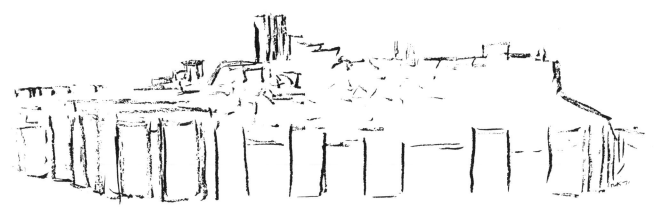

The City from a simple settlement became the place of the assembled Institutions

Before the Institution was natural agreement — the sense of common ability. A mule foothold is confiden in the settlement — The first institution The constant play of circumstances, from moment to moment unpredictable distort Inspiring beginnings of natural agreement.

The measure of the greatness of a place to live must come from the character of its Institutions sanctioned thru how sensitive they are to renewed. and Desire for new Agreement

(not need because it comes from us, Desire is the thing not made the roots of the will to live

The Street

In a city the street must be supreme. It is the first institution of the city. The street is a room by agreement, a community room, the walls of which belong to the donors, dedicated to the city for common use. Its ceiling is the sky. From the street must have come the meeting house, also a place by agreement.

Today, streets are disinterested movements not at all belonging to the houses that front them. So you have no streets. You have roads, but you have no streets.

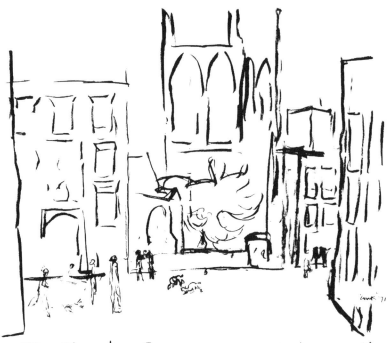

The Street is a Room by agreement A community Room the walls of which belong to the donors dedicated to the city for common use Its ceiling is the sky From The street must have come The Meeting House also a place by agreement

The School

I think of school as an environment of spaces where it is good to learn. Schools began with a man under a tree, who did not know he was a teacher, discussing his realization with a few, who did not know they were students. The students aspired that their sons also listen to such a man. Spaces were erected and the first schools became. It can also be said that the existence-will of school was there even before the circumstances of the man under a tree. That is why it is good for the mind to go back to the beginning, because the beginning of any established activity is its most wonderful moment.

You get an order from the school board that says, "We have a great idea. We should not put windows in the school, because the children need wall space for their paintings, and also windows can distract from the teacher." Now, what teacher deserves that much attention? I'd like to know. Because after all, the bird outside, the person scurrying for shelter in the rain, the leaves falling from the tree, the clouds passing by, the sun penetrating: these are all great things. They are lessons in themselves.

Windows are essential to the school. You are made from light, and therefore you must live with the sense that light is important. Such a direction from the school board telling you what life is all about must be resisted. Without light there is no architecture.

The Chapel

In understanding the nature of a chapel, I said first you have a sanctuary, and the sanctuary is for those who want to kneel. Around the sanctuary is an ambulatory, and the ambulatory is for those who are not sure, but who want to be near. Outside is a court for those who want to feel the presence of the chapel. And the court has a wall. Those who pass the wall can just wink at it.

Architecture

I thought that Art was a kind of oracle, an aura that had to be satisfied by the artist. If the artist made something, he dedicated it as an offering to Art, as though Art were something that preceded the work. Art cannot be Art unless it is a work and not something abstract, out in the blue somewhere. The emergence of architecture as a human expression is tremendously important because we actually live to express.

A great building, in my opinion, must begin with the unmeasurable, must go through measurable means when it is being designed, and in the end must be unmeasurable. The only way you can build, the only way you can get the building into being, is through the measurable. You must follow the laws of nature and use quantities of brick, methods of construction, and engineering. But in the end, when the building becomes part of living, it evokes unmeasurable qualities, and the spirit of its existence takes over.

Architecture has existence, but it has no presence. Only a work of architecture has presence, and a work of architecture is presented as an offering to architecture.

A work is made in the urging sounds of industry, and, when the dust settles, the pyramid, echoing Silence, gives the sun its shadow.

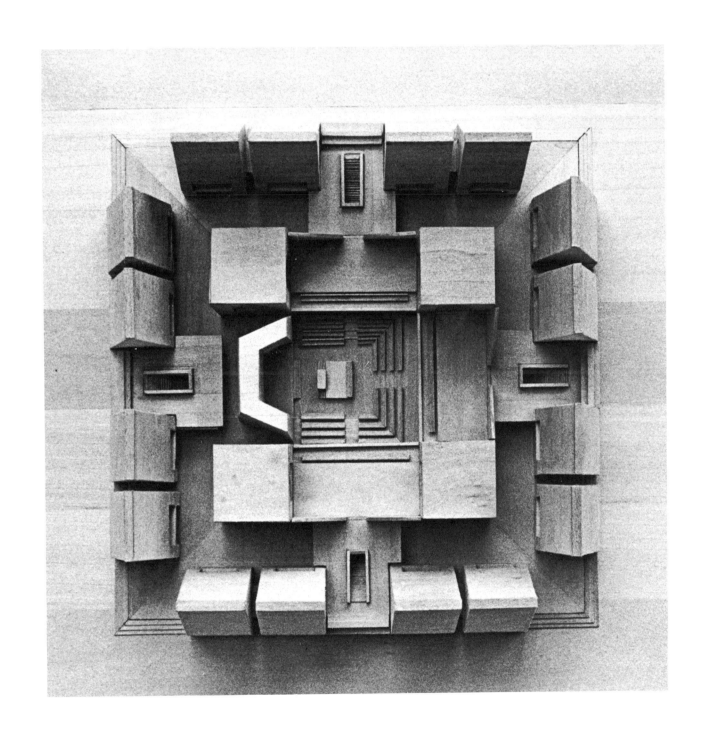

The Architect

The way one does things is private, but what one does can belong to everybody. Your greatest worth is in the area where you can claim no ownership, and the part that you do that doesn't belong to you is the most precious. It is the kind of thing you can offer because it is a better part of you; it is a part of general commonality that belongs to everybody. You feel that what you truly have to offer is in your next work, and that what you have done is always incomplete. I believe that even a great composer like Bach, who did everything as though it belonged to everyone else, died thinking he did nothing, because a person is greater than his works. He must continue.

I believe it takes a long time to be an architect; it takes a long time to be the architect of one's aspirations. You can become an architect professionally overnight. But to feel the spirit of architecture from which one makes his offering takes much longer.

And where does the architect sit? He sits right there; he is the one who conveys the beauty of spaces, which is the very meaning of architecture. Think of meaningful space and you invent an environment, and it can be your invention. Therein lies the architect.

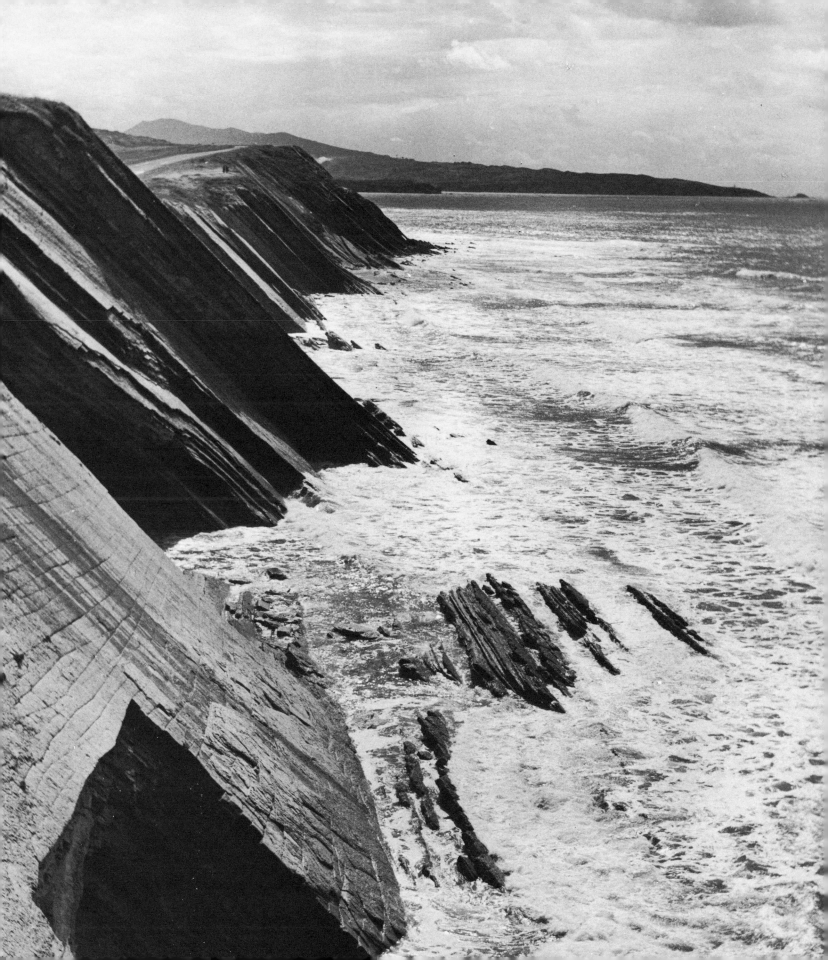

The Teacher

I must reflect on the mystery of circumstances that lead a man into paths which he could not have anticipated. I was to be a painter. There was no question about it, until my last year in high school when a course on architecture hit me so strongly, I knew I would be an architect. The course concerned the earliest architecture: Greek, Roman, Romanesque, Gothic, Renaissance. I felt a great happiness. I had no question as to what my career would be. I had no idea, of course, of modern architecture. Now, though we are living in the field of modern architecture, I feel a closer association to this marvelous architecture of the past than I do to the architecture of today. It is constantly in my mind as a reference. I say to this architecture, "How am I doing, Gothic architecture? How am I doing, Greek architecture?"

Everyone has a figure in his work to whom he feels answerable. I also say to myself, "How am I doing, Corbusier?" You see, Corbusier was my teacher, and Paul Cret was my teacher. I have learned not to *do* as they did, not to imitate, but to sense their spirit.

The work of students should not be directed to the solution of problems, but rather to sensing the nature of a thing. But you cannot know a nature without getting it out of your guts. You must *sense* what it is, and then you can look up what other people think it is. What you sense must belong to you, and the words of teaching must not in any way be in evidence, so completely has it been transformed into the singularity.

When I talk to students, the one feeling I always have is that every one of them can surpass me in my work. They don't, but my attitude is that being in school is like being in a chapel, and my duty is to write psalms. I come refreshed and self-challenged from the classroom. I learn more from the students than I teach. This is not an idle thing. It is not what they teach me, but what I teach myself in the presence of singularities. Teaching is an act of singularity to singularity. It is not talking to a group. They teach you of your own singularity, because only a singularity can teach a singularity.

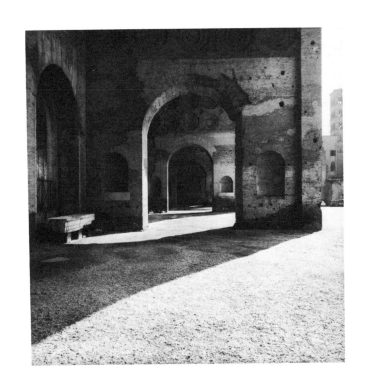

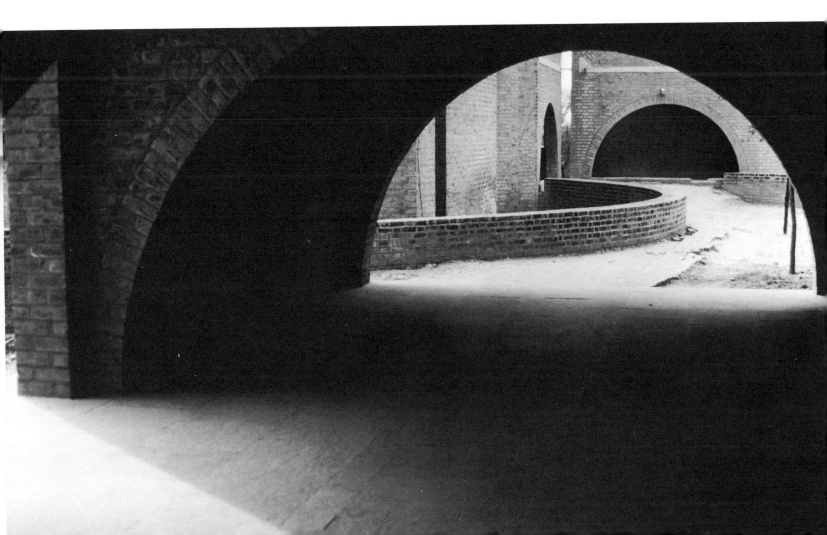

Time Beyond Time

I have, in my place, books about English history. I like the bloodiness of it. I have one set of eight volumes. I read only the first volume, and of that only the first chapter, in which each time I see something else. But really, I am interested only in reading Volume Zero, which has not been written. And then volume minus one. History could not have started in the places they speak of. History preceded this; it just is not recorded. The beauty of architecture is that it deals with the recessions of the mind, from which comes that which is not yet said and not yet made.

Of all things, I honor beginnings. I believe, though, that what was has always been, and what is has always been, and what will be has always been. I do not think the circumstantial play from year to year, from era to era, has anything to do with what is available to you. The person of old had the same brilliance of mind that we assume we have now. But that which made a thing become manifest for the first time is our great moment of creative happening.

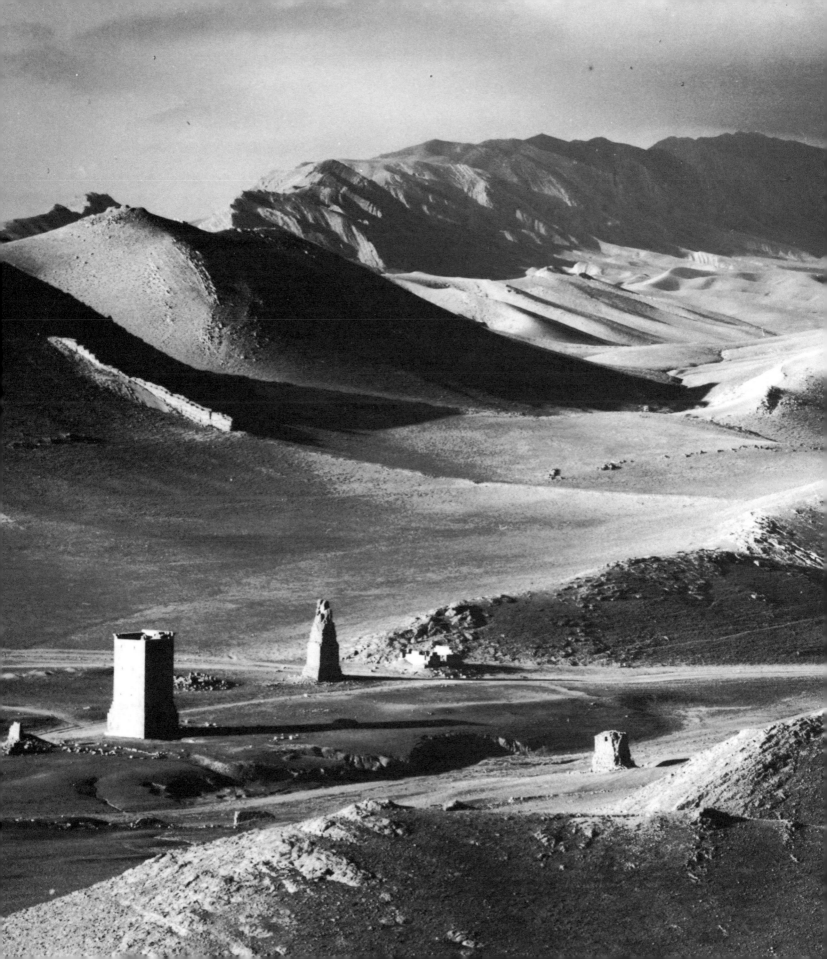

Why Architecture?

STUDENT: Why architecture?

KAHN: I think that if you were to define it, you would destroy it. In a Hebraic way of attacking your logical problem, I ask you one question. Maybe you can answer it. I would say that if you ask your question as, "Why anything?" maybe the answer is in that.

STUDENT: Because it is.

KAHN: Yes. Exactly. Because it is.

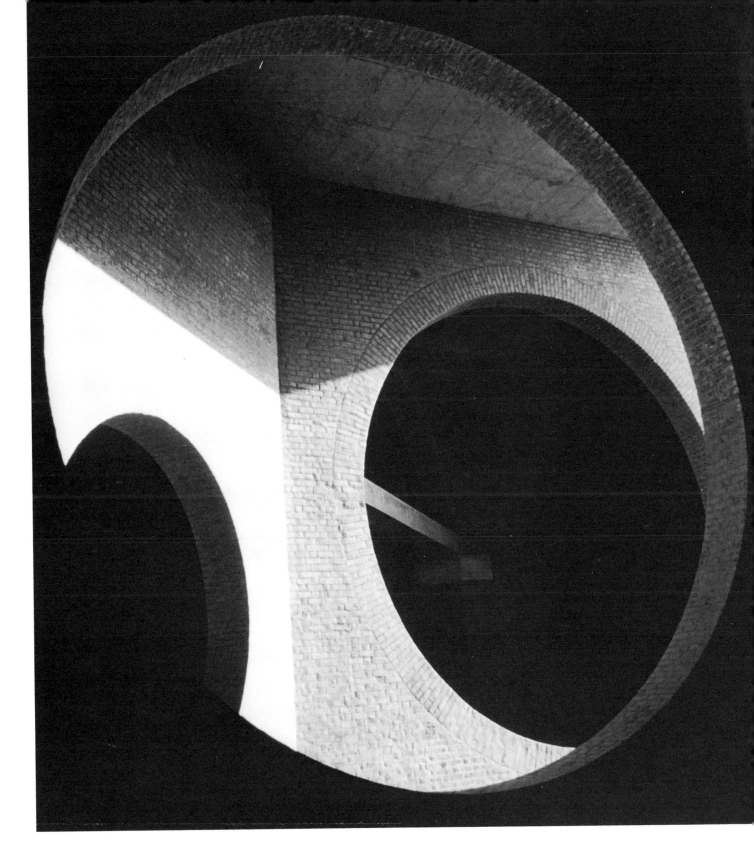

Architecture as Spirit

Architecture

Architecture is the manifestation in form of the order of our experience. It is a model of our consciousness, the fitting of ourselves between the earth and the sky, the patterns in which we relate one to another, and the physical presence of our institutions. The architecture of each culture is a model of that culture's world, not of the world's shape, but of its underlying form. Thus, we do not directly see in modern architecture the expanding universe that some scientists describe, nor do we see in Hindu architecture the great disc, set on the backs of four elephants, standing on a giant tortoise swimming in an endless sea—which the Hindus once thought of as their world. Rather, we find in architecture a model of the underlying principles that govern the world, the forces that give it shape and the space and time for its action. It is in this light that we can see, for example, a Gothic cathedral as a great model of the Medieval universe, depicting the boundaries of the human act, comings and goings on Earth and in heaven, the nature of material and of light, the forces of nature, and the human and divine wills as they were experienced in the Middle Ages.

In *The Decline of the West* [35], Oswald Spengler described the architectures of each of several cultures as expressions of their worldviews. Spengler saw the ancient Egyptian moving down a narrow and prescribed life-path that continued into and through death to end before the judges of the dead. There was no consideration of deviation to either side of the path, as nothing existed other than the path. The great Egyptian temples were a rhythmically ordered sequence of spaces, the sacred way leading through avenues of rams or sphinxes to the massive temple gates, and then through arcaded courts, pillared rooms, and halls to a sacred chamber. Similarly, the pyramid presented a triangular stone surface that defined the way across the desert from any

direction. Life proceeded guided by the flat smooth stone surfaces of an austere architecture.

The Egyptian directional movement contrasted to the flowing Chinese Way, following the principle of Tao. The Chinese wandered through the world unrestricted by stone walls, moving through nature. The Chinese temple was not a self-contained building, but rather a complex that included hills, water, trees, flowers, and stones, as well as the building itself, which let space flow through it like the breeze.

The Greek experienced the differentiation of the individual from society and from nature. The evolution of the statue of the standing nude youth shows the emergence of this bodily self. The magical forces evident in the archaic figures give way to anatomical idealism and individual expression in Classical and Hellenic figures. For the Greeks, presence was immediate, not abstracted through space or time. Greek vase painting had no depth; the characters in Greek drama, no psychological change over time; and the Greek temple, no useful interior. The temple was freestanding against the landscape, its Doric columns perfect in proportion, standing erect, free, and apart.

The Gothic cathedral prefigured the coursing movement of Western consciousness through space. The continuous change in the calculus, the elliptical orbits of the planets, the complex tones of Baroque music, and the emotional depth of Rembrandt's paintings could all be seen in the spatial depth of the Gothic cathedral. It was lofty and almost without walls, a stone cage with vaults whose forces sprang up at their joinings, its flying buttresses carrying forces from the cool interior out to the sun, and its stained glass bringing the sun, transformed to luminous color, inside. Escaping the concreteness of the body, the Western experience eventually soared in the abstraction of pure space and time, down into the haze of sub-atomic particles and out into the infinite reaches of a pulsating universe.

To know the world, the architects of each period turned both inward and outward. The Egyptian, the Chinese, the Greek, and the Gothic architect each found what was for a time a clarity before the world again became a flux. The Renaissance architect, Alberti, upon mastering the art of perspective, exclaimed, "At last I can see the world as God sees it!" Indeed, for that moment, Alberti had captured the world in a crystalline space defined by converging lines of perspective. We saw in perspective, and the world existed in uniform space and time from the fifteenth until the beginning of the twentieth century. Then, the physics of Einstein, the canvases of the Cubists, the novels of Proust and Joyce, and the open plan of Frank Lloyd Wright's architecture set the world again into flux, to emerge in a relativistic, existential space-time. The architect, like the artist, the poet, and the scientist, is the vehicle through which form continually comes into the world, created anew.

Modern Architecture

Modern architecture is an expression of the rational worldview that began to emerge during the Renaissance as a reaction against the Medieval institutions of church, empire, and feudalism. In place of these institutions, Renaissance thinkers placed the human being, which they designated the measure of all things. They proposed that the human being was a creature of nature, capable of understanding both itself and nature with the tools of mathematics, rational thought, and the senses. Mathematics was the language of nature; rational thought, the language of the mind; and the senses, the link between the two. Newton's use of mathematics in the seventeenth century to describe both earthly mechanics and the motions of celestial bodies lent great support to the rationalist view. In the eighteenth century,

during the Enlightenment, rationalism was extended from the natural sciences to human affairs, where it played a role in the American and French Revolutions. By the nineteenth century the Industrial Revolution had seemingly confirmed the powers of rationalism not only to understand nature but also to conquer nature. With Marx and Freud, rationalism was extended to human history and to human consciousness, and by the early twentieth century, it dominated architecture and the arts.

Rationalism is expressed in modern architecture in two ways: first, through functionalism; and second, through abstract rectilinear shapes. All architecture is functional if it serves its intended purpose, but in the late nineteenth and early twentieth century, functionalism took on a specific meaning: an architecture that fulfilled its direct utilitarian purposes and no others. This definition served to deny the legitimacy of any ornament or references to past historical styles. Of course, an ornamented building can serve utilitarian purposes just as well as an unornamented building, but the elimination of historical styles was part of the agenda of modern architects, and functionalism was used to give that agenda a moral legitimacy.

Functionalism was promoted through the design of modern buildings from a program. Previously buildings had been designed from prototypes, that is, from basic building types that had proven serviceable in the past and that carried certain symbolic meanings. A prototype was chosen and adapted to a particular set of circumstances. In designing from a program, the architect starts not with a prototype but with a list of activities, their spatial requirements, and their relationships to one another. This list leads to diagrams of spaces and relationships, which then lead to the shapes of the building. Functionalist theory holds that there should be no influence on the design of a building other than the program, the conditions of the site, and the nature of the materials to be used in the construction of the building.

This approach is designed to assure that those intangibles, such as the human spirit, which cannot be expressed in a list of requirements, will not be considered. According to this theory, if the proper method is followed, a building with a beauty similar to that of a machine will result. It is also held that the betterment of human society will follow from an architecture that serves identifiable physical human needs as listed in the program.

Of course, architects do not strictly adhere to functionalism; it would probably be impossible to do so. Equally as influential on modern architecture has been the aesthetic of abstract rectilinear shapes. This aesthetic became particularly pronounced in the 1920s and is still with us today. Like functionalism, this aesthetic has served to dissociate modern architecture from the styles of the past. It also was intended to symbolize the regularity and repetitiveness of modern industrialized materials and construction techniques, although such materials and techniques do not necessarily dictate rectilinear buildings. The dissociation of modern architecture from the styles of the past was not just a by-product of other objectives but also an end in itself. The modern architects believed that the tools of rationalism had made possible a scientific and universal architecture beyond all past styles, based on mathematics and the immutable laws of nature.

There were reactions against rationalism during the course of its development in architecture and in other fields, but on the whole, its development was steady. The rational worldview might be described as a vision of a great clockwork universe of uniform space and time in which motion was governed by mathematical laws. All was knowable, and ultimately all would be known. From the time of the Renaissance through the mid-nineteenth century, this crystalline vision was as valid for the West as were the visions of the Egyptians or the Greeks for their times. But in the late nineteenth century, just as absolute rigor in all of the sciences seemed obtainable, the underlying foundations of the rational worldview began to crumble. Experiments to determine the Earth's absolute motion through space revealed disquieting results, and eventually Einstein's special and general relativity did away with uniform space and time. Later, quantum mechanics undermined causality. Worse still, mathematics, which had seemed the absolute and stable fulcrum between consciousness and the world, began to give way. First, non-Euclidian geometries began to suggest that mathematics might not have an *a priori* validity. Then, in 1931, Gödel published his proofs demonstrating the necessary incompleteness and inconsistency of all mathematical systems [31].

The ability of science to adequately account for the human experience of the world has been called into doubt from many sides. At the same time as the modern movement in architecture was looking to the physical sciences as a model for an objective science of architecture, the physical sciences themselves were retreating from objectivity. In the early twentieth century, Frank Lloyd Wright recognized the necessity of transcending rationalism in architecture, but the modern European architects who gained ascendency in the 1920s still sought a rational rigor. After the Second World War, these Europeans dominated architecture. By the late 1950s their rigor could no longer hold, and the glass box, which once held promise of a crystal city, was spreading a blight of anonymity, alienation, and sterility to cities throughout the world.

Rationality is a discipline for understanding things that are. However, if we attempt to see a larger world, one that includes *that which is not yet* along with *that which is,* as the creative artist, scientist, and architect must, then a more powerful discipline is needed, one used by the poets, which the ancient Chinese Taoist philosopher Lao Tzu called the Tao, the existential philosopher Martin Heidegger called Being, and Louis Kahn called Order.

Order

Louis Kahn was educated in the 1920s at the University of Pennsylvania in the Beaux-Arts tradition. The Beaux-Arts was a system of education dating back to the beginning of the nineteenth century, originally developed in France and strongly grounded in the classical orders of Greece and Rome. At the heart of the Beaux-Arts was the assumption that our culture achieved its solidity through its classical foundations. This classical view survived into the twentieth century in parallel with the modern movement in architecture, but by the 1940s it was no longer tenable and was abandoned. In the 1930s Kahn became involved with modern architecture, but he was never fully comfortable with it. From his education, he knew that there was a deeper order to be found beyond rationalism. It could no longer be found by returning to old styles as the Beaux-Arts had done. It would have to be found by going into and beyond rationalism.

Kahn struggled for years in his search for order. At first he thought he was seeking more solid organizing principles for his architecture. Eventually he realized that he was seeking a general principle, one which would apply to all of existence. At that time he began to speak of Order.

Order became Kahn's means of finding the human place in the world, the nature of our consciousness, and the relationship of our consciousness to nature. Rationalism had separated consciousness and nature, with mathematics as their common link. Order placed them together, each dependent on the other. Kahn did not say what Order is, but spoke of it in metaphor. Order is the principle behind all things and is expressed in them as an existence-will, a quality things have in their beginnings outside of time, which Kahn liked to call Volume Zero. We might also say that Order is, not only an underlying principle and a quality of things, but also an active creativity: it is the way things come into being. This understanding of Order is necessary so that we do not limit or diminish its meaning, for Order pertains not only to things that are, but also to things that are not yet. In human consciousness it is the creative force that takes an active role in making through art what nature does not make. Order is ultimately beyond description, and eventually Kahn said simply, "Order is."

There is an Order of all things: of wind, of materials, of our being. Kahn was in touch with Order in two ways. The first was by direct questioning. This can be seen in his conversation with the brick, which begins, "Brick, what do you like?" He explains that you can have the same conversation with any material, or with nature itself. Kahn begins the design of a building in a similar way with the question, "What does this building want to be?" The second way in which Kahn was in touch with Order was by looking into himself. Order governs the making of everything that is made, and in every thing is the record of its making. The record of our making is in our intuition. Intuition is, therefore, our truest sense. In consulting his intuition about his own origins, Kahn uncovered the "genesis" from Joy to Silence and Light. He understood genesis or creation to be not only something that took place in the past, but something that takes place at every moment. Since it takes place also at this moment, creation is something we have direct access to, something in which we can participate.

While the Order of which Kahn spoke is not subject to direct description, it can be described through poetic metaphor. In speaking of Order, Kahn called that which does not yet exist, Silence. That which exists, he called Light. Silence is the unmeasurable, the desire to be.

Light is the measurable, the giver of presence. Between Silence and Light is a threshold over which movement takes place from one to the other. The language of this threshold, which Kahn called the Treasury of Shadow, is art. Art is the means whereby something moves from Silence to Light. Thus, if we were to ask where a building or any work of art is before it is brought into existence by the architect or the artist, the answer is that it is in the realm of Silence. The task of the architect is to first bring it from Silence to Light, that is, bring it into Realization, and then bring it from Light into material, that is, from Realization into the actual building.

Kahn understood that the duality of Silence and Light is only apparent. He said that he saw them as brothers, realizing that actually there were not two, or even one. Beyond duality is oneness, and beyond oneness there is still something, which Kahn called Order.

Kahn used the word Light to mean pure being, as yet without material quality. He observed that material begins where light (using the word in its ordinary sense) stops. In making an architectural drawing, he saw that the place where he made a line was where the light was not. When the building was built, the line became the wall, also where the light stopped. He said, "All of the material world is Light that has spent itself."

Light (again using the word in its ordinary sense) is of immense importance to architecture; it is the revealer of architecture. The great modern architect, Le Corbusier, wrote [3], "Architecture is the correct and magnificent play of masses brought together in light." If we compare the classical architecture of places with differing light, for example, the architecture of Greece, with its intense sunlight, to the architecture of England, with its hazy light, we see how important light is in the making of buildings.

The great historical architectures were built in masonry, which necessitated thick walls. Openings in these walls reflected the light from their sides and sculpted the light as it entered the room. Modern architecture, with the sophistication of its thin materials, does not provide such modulation of light. Much of Kahn's effort in design was to recapture the means, using the materials of modern architecture, to again sculpt light before bringing it into a room.

Kahn's concept of Order is in many ways similar to Lao Tzu's concept of the Tao. Lao Tzu wrote [34]:

> The Tao that can be told is not the eternal Tao.
> The name that can be named is not the eternal name.
> The nameless is the beginning of heaven and earth.
> The named is the mother of the ten thousand things.
> Ever desireless, one can see the mystery.
> Ever desiring, one can see the manifestations .

What Kahn called Silence, Lao Tzu called the nameless. What Kahn called Light, Lao Tzu called the named. Elsewhere, Lao Tzu referred to being and not being, and he wrote:

> The ten thousand things are born of being.
> Being is born of not being.

Kahn said that Light condenses to form the material world. Lao Tzu called the material world "the ten thousand things," which come from the named, or from being.

Kahn felt that Order lies beyond the apparent duality of Silence and Light. Lao Tzu wrote:

> The Tao begot one.
> One begot two.
> Two begot three.
> And three begot the ten thousand things.

In making reference to similarities between Kahn's and Lao Tzu's poetry, I should also point out differences between the two men, which might be characterized as distinctions between traditional Eastern and Western modes of existence. These are illustrated in Frank Lloyd

Wright's encounter with Eastern thought. Although there are differences in Kahn's and Wright's philosophy and architecture, they shared a common spirit and drive to create. Wright had developed what he called organic architecture in response to democracy, the openness of the American landscape and the availability of modern materials. Wright saw similarities between his organic philosophy and Oriental thought. He wrote [4]:

> But it is not so much the principles of this [Buddhist] faith which underlie organic architecture, as the faith of Laotse [Lao Tzu]—the Chinese philosopher. . . . But I became conscious of these only after I had found and built it for myself. . . . For a long time, I thought I had "discovered" it, only to find after all that this idea of the interior space being the reality of the building was ancient and Oriental. . . . When pretty well puffed up by this I received a little book by Okakura Kakuzo, entitled *The Book of Tea,* sent to me by the ambassador from Japan to the United States. Reading it, I came across this sentence, "The reality of a room was to be found in the space enclosed by the roof and walls, not in the roof and walls themselves."
>
> Well, there was I. Instead of being the cake I was not even dough. Closing the little book I went out to break stone on the road, trying to get my interior self together. I was like a sail coming down; I had thought of myself as an original, but was not. It took me days to swell up again. But I began to swell up again when I thought, "After all, who built it? Who put that thought into buildings? Laotse nor anyone had consciously *built* it." When I thought of that, naturally enough I thought, "Well then, everything is all right, we can still go along with head up." I have been going along—head up—ever since.

We see in Wright a strong sense of personal ego, an emphasis on the accomplishments of the individual, and the value of the building as a cultural monument, a work of art. This we find also in Louis Kahn. If perhaps the ultimate intention for Wright and Lao Tzu is the same, certainly the emphasis is different. Lao Tzu's goal was the realization of the Tao; it is the ultimate; all worldly accomplishments pale beside it. Wright and Kahn, however, could not be satisfied with finding organic space or Order. Each felt compelled to engage what he found, wrestle with it, and bring it into circumstantial expression in this world with his personal stamp on it. The artist is driven to create but is never fully satisfied with his or her creations. Kahn said that even Bach, who was undeniably a great composer, must have died thinking he did nothing. Your greatest work is always your next; you must continue, and even death cannot satisfactorily conclude your struggle.

Institutions

The metaphor of Silence and Light told Kahn how a building comes into existence. His understanding of human institutions told him what a building serves.

We tend today to regard institutions negatively. We think of large, bureaucratic, unresponsive organizations that are more concerned with their own growth than with serving human needs. But Kahn saw that behind these institutions are desires, such as the desire to learn, which can be expressed only in community, through people coming together. Kahn felt that service to these human desires remains faintly present in our institutions today, and that architecture can serve those desires. For Kahn, architecture is the art whose concern is human institutions. Buildings are not mere abstract forms; they are always for an institution: the house is for residence, the school building for learning, the laboratory for science, etc. A building can be meaningful only in serving a vital institution.

Institutions grow out of the defining quality of human being, which is the desire to express oneself. It is this desire that makes us human. Kahn said [18],

"Desire—the qualities of the not yet said and the not yet made—is the reason for living. It is the core of the expressive instinct and must never be stymied."

For Kahn, desire is the avenue of expression, and there are three great desires: the desire to learn, the desire to meet together, and the desire for well-being. Acting through their common will, people sought to meet these desires, and they formed the first institutions: the school, the street, and the village green. All of our institutions today refer back to these beginnings. It is important to note again that by beginnings, Kahn did not mean historical beginnings, but rather eternal beginnings outside of time.

A building can and should house the spirit of its institution, even if its immediate users have forgotten it. Teachers may become bureaucratic; legislators, corrupt; and clergy, dogmatic. But the halls of the school can always be there to enable people to exchange ideas; the chambers of the legislature can be there to enable people to gather in community; and the vaults of the church can be there to aid in one's communication with God. It is not the measurable in the building, not anything from the list of functions and spaces in the client's program, that can do these things. It is the architect's realization of the original intention of the school, the legislature, and the church, expressed in the building, that keeps before us the institution's human-serving purpose.

Kahn's most important work was done during the 1960s and the early 1970s, a time of disruption and questioning of institutions. Many architects felt either that institutions must be changed and that architecture must be suspended until that change was accomplished, or that change was not possible and that architecture should withdraw into formal aesthetics, ignoring the institutional use to which it would be put. Kahn rejected both of these attitudes, one as utopian and the other as nihilistic. For Kahn, architecture meant continuous engagement in the real world as it exists at the moment, using the circumstantial, that is the specific building, its uses and materials, as a means of reaching back into the eternal to bring new Realizations into being, thereby enriching the world.

Form and Design

Kahn distinguished between Form and Design. Usually by form we mean physical shape or artistic order. However, Kahn used Form to mean an existence-will, the nature of a thing previous to its physical reality. An existence-will is in everything; it expresses the Order of a thing. A rose wants to be a rose; a human being wants to be a human being. Kahn's concept of the existence-will is similar to that of the nineteenth-century philosopher, Arthur Schopenhauer, who felt that everything in nature, including human being, is an objectification of will. Since this is true of both ourselves and of the objects we perceive, we can know the workings of will through introspection. Art held a special place in Schopenhauer's philosophy, and he regarded music as the direct expression of the will. Architecture has been called frozen music.

It is the role of the architect to discover the existence-will of a building and to bring it into the circumstantial world. Kahn would always start with the question: "What does this building want to be?" The answer to this question would yield the Form.

In the case of a chapel, the Form might be seen in Kahn's statement [19]:

> First you have a sanctuary and the sanctuary is for those who want to kneel. Around the sanctuary is an ambulatory, and the ambulatory is for those who are not sure but who want to be near. Outside is a court for those who want to feel the presence of the chapel. And the court has a wall. Those who pass the wall can just wink at it.

In this case the Form is expressed in words. It might also be expressed as a diagram.

Kahn's approach of starting with Form was quite different from the approach of most modern architects, who, as discussed earlier, start with a program of activities and spaces. Kahn's first reaction to the program given to him by the client was to change it. It could never tell him what he needed to know in order to design a building that would be an offering to its institution. Thus, he said that if a school board requests a school without windows, the architect must resist. Light is essential to life, to learning, and therefore to the Form of the school. Once the Form is sensed, the architect can begin Design. Design gives the Form specific shape and materials, and brings it into the circumstantial world. The design process also involves a play back and forth, a testing of the Form in the Design, and the development of a new Form if necessary. But Design cannot begin without the Form.

Kahn felt that Form is impersonal; it belongs to the building. But Design belongs to the architect. Kahn's contribution to architecture was in Design as well as in Form. As mentioned earlier, modern architects had sought to cut architecture off from the past through the use of abstract rectilinear shapes that would produce buildings not recognizable in terms of previous architectural styles. Kahn's approach was different. He reestablished a contact with the past through his buildings because he felt that the great historical architectures of Egypt, Greece, and particularly Rome—which has been a source for Western architecture for two thousand years—were closer to the beginnings of architecture and of human institutions, and therefore were more vital than modern architecture.

Past architectures had a reverence for materials, which were taken directly from nature and translated through the human creative consciousness into architecture. The Industrial Revolution had separated the architect from the processes of construction, and materials had lost their special qualities. Kahn reintroduced this reverence. The depth of Kahn's investigation of materials can be seen in his conversation with the brick. In his work he used brick, concrete, slate, teak, oak, lead, travertine, and steel with a freshness that has renewed the vitality of these materials in our architecture. Also from the past, Kahn reintroduced a concern for the human place in the world. He stressed the connection between form and human meaning in architecture. We see this in his emphasis on structure as the organizer of human experience, and specifically in such ideas as the place of the column as the giver of Order.

Kahn also learned from the great modern architects. From Mies van der Rohe, he learned the richness obtainable in the sparse and austere use of materials and the use of structure to order space. From Le Corbusier, Kahn learned the use of form to respond to the human act. And although he personally did not admire Frank Lloyd Wright's architecture, Wright provided a model for the remaking of architecture from the beginning [28]. At times, Kahn integrated the discoveries of these men into his own work, but primarily he tried, as he said, to feel their spirit. Similarly, some of the younger architects who have responded to Kahn's influence have done so by applying the depth of his investigations to uniquely contemporary problems, being sensitive to his investigations of Form, but pursuing their own Designs.

Kahn's concepts of the eternal and of Form are similar to what Carl Jung called the collective unconscious and the archetypes. For Jung, the collective unconscious is a realm of being that transcends the individual unconscious and is made up of archetypes, which are patterns or forms embodying the eternal themes of human experience. The manifestation of these themes varies according to the idiom and the circumstances of a particular culture. Thus, the dying and the resurrecting god is an archetype that achieves expression in Osiris, Dionysius, Christ, etc. Similarly, for Kahn, the school is an eternal Form that achieves expression in a particular school building, which responds to its place and time, but also is an offering to learning.

Where Architecture Serves

Kahn distinguished between desire and need. He said [18], "It is disgraceful not to supply needs, and it goes without saying that if you are brought into this world, your needs must be supplied. But desire is infinitely more important than need." As citizens we all have responsibilities toward need. The primary purpose of architecture for Kahn was not social reform or urban renewal, but in his work, Kahn did address social and economic problems. He designed low income housing and was sensitive to appropriate technologies, using sophisticated post-tensioned concrete in the United States, but bricks in capitally poor, labor-rich Bangladesh and India. However, several dozen buildings, the efforts of one architect, can not appreciably benefit a country if they respond only to need. If architecture is to be of service, it must respond to more than need. The architect must also serve desire; the desire of the building to be what it wants to be and the desire of the human being for self-expression.

In serving desire, architecture contributes to the spiritual enrichment of the world. This enrichment takes place through the opening of a passage between Silence and Light. Through this passage, the unmeasurable can move into the measurable, and as the building stands and holds open the passage, we can have access back to the unmeasurable. Kahn felt that a great building begins with a Realization in the unmeasurable. This Realization comes from the architect's search for beginnings—of institutions, of materials, of all things that are made. The Realization is intangible and must then be brought over the threshold from the unmeasurable into the measurable, first as Form, and then as a material building. The measurable includes bricks and concrete, and also clients, budgets, building codes, and contractors. When all of these have been consulted and respected without losing the original Realization, a great building can emerge. Then, standing before the Parthenon, in the nave of Chartres Cathedral, or in the open court of Kahn's Salk Institute, we can experience access back into the unmeasurable, and can thereby be more complete in ourselves and more fully in the world. Kahn said [17], "A work is made in the urging sounds of industry, and when the dust settles, the pyramid, echoing Silence, gives the sun its shadow."

Of course, architecture is not always seen in this way. It is often regarded purely as the making of buildings and as a profession. For Kahn, architecture was a spiritual path. Kahn said [18]:

> There are many possibilities that are still in the air that we can make happen. The architect's job, in my opinion, is to find ways that the availabilities that are not yet here can have spaces, and those that are here already can have better environments for their maturing into that which talks to you. The spaces that you make must be the seat of a certain offering of a person to the next person. It is not an operational thing; you can leave that to the builders and the operators. Already they are building eighty-five percent of the architecture, so give them another five percent. Take only ten percent, or five percent, and be *really* an architect, not a professional. The professional will bury you. You become so comparable. You will be praised so equally to someone else that you will never recognize yourself. You will become good in business, you will play golf all day, and your buildings will be built anyway. But what the devil is that and what kind of living is that? What Joy is there if Joy is buried? I think Joy is the key word in our work. It must be felt. If you don't feel Joy in what you're doing, then you're

not really alive. There are miserable moments you have to live through, but really, Joy will prevail.

What Kahn had to teach about architecture should be applicable to any discipline. A discipline, the activity we choose for our lives, should engage us in our culture and should enable us to give something that can be received by others. A discipline will not present itself to us in this way. We must make it so for ourselves.

The Human Place

What is the human place in the Order that Kahn described? Kahn saw human being as a unique meeting of the measurable and the unmeasurable. This meeting can be seen in the play between knowledge, which is measurable, and intuition, which is unmeasurable; between the brain, which we get potluck from nature and is circumstantial, and the Spirit, which is eternal. Because of this meeting in us of the measurable and the unmeasurable, we have a special role to play bringing things from Silence to Light, with art as the language of that role and therefore the true human language.

The philosopher Martin Heidegger, whose work is central to contemporary existential thought, had a view of existence and of human being similar to Kahn's. What Kahn called Order and Lao Tzu called the Tao, Heidegger called Being. For Heidegger, Being is the ground through which all things are [33]. The human calling is to watch over Being and to act as a shepherd for Being. Heidegger felt that we have neglected this calling and that we have become cut off from Being, a condition that dates back to ancient Greece. For Parmenides, Being and thought were one, but for Aristotle, the two became separated, and the human became an animal that has rational thought but is torn from the ground of Being.

Heidegger saw a "darkening of the world" as we become more and more interested in research, that is, in manageable, planned, systematic tasks, at the expense of insight and understanding. We have abandoned our role as shepherds for Being. Kahn would say that we are concerned with the measurable and have neglected Order. Lao Tzu would say that we are concerned with the ten thousand things and have neglected the Tao. Heidegger saw two disastrous consequences in our abandonment of our calling. One is that Being itself has become, in Nietzsche's phrase, "a haze." It has suffered from our neglect, and we no longer have a sense that it exists. The other is that we ourselves have become lost. We wander through life overwhelmed by the myriad details of the material world, but we have no sense of what stands beyond that world and what our place might be in a larger scheme of things.

The human place at the Treasury of the Shadow is tenuous. To maintain it, the scientist must act out of intouchness with nature, the physician must seek wholeness, the craftsman must be at one with material, the poet must speak Being, and the architect must seek Order.

Architecture in stone began with Imhotep, the ancient Egyptian architect of the first pyramid, inventor of civilization, high priest, and later, god of healing. It is interesting that the Egyptians saw their first architect also as a healer. The bringing of wholeness to the culture and to the person were seen as one. The titles of architects have varied over history: in Egypt, a priest-healer; in Gothic France, a chief artisan; in Renaissance Italy, an artist-engineer. But the role remains the same; to watch over Being, to search for Order, and to renew culture through the manifestation of Spirit in form.

The architect is directly engaged in the circumstantial in building with materials and in making history. A great architect recognizes the circumstantial changes in a culture and embodies that change in buildings. By this measure, Kahn was a great architect. But there is another kind of measure, one that transcends a particular time, for architects who design only for their own time must also be limited by that time. Kahn also explored the eternal in nature, in humanity, and in architecture. He designed his buildings in response to beginnings outside of time, as well as the immediate uses called for by his clients. A great building is built with the recognition that uses change over the years and over the centuries, but that deep parts of human being do not change. A great building tells those who first use it the meaning of their age, and to those of the future, it tells the stories of its past. And it tells all people about the eternal beyond time. It was by being in touch with the eternal that Kahn achieved a greatness far beyond that which can be accorded by any given time. Kahn was in touch with the Tao of architecture.

Commenting on our culture, T. S. Eliot wrote [32]:

> Between the idea
> And the reality
> Between the motion
> And the Act
> Falls the Shadow

Louis Kahn taught us to understand the Order of the Shadow—what lies between idea and reality, between Silence and Light.

Some of Louis Kahn's Buildings

As long as any of his buildings stand, and most of them will stand a long, long time, Lou will be speaking directly to the living humans whom he loved and who all loved him. When his buildings are gone, forever after, humans will benefit through this indirectly assimilated wisdom.

Buckminster Fuller

Alfred Newton Richards Medical Research Buildings

3700 Hamilton Walk, University of Pennsylvania
Philadelphia, Pennsylvania

1957-61

The Medical Towers, which Kahn started in his late fifties, was his first building of major importance. In its functionalism, response to program, honesty in use of materials, and use of glass, the building is a culmination of modern architecture. At the same time it transcends modern architecture and becomes the beginning of something new.

In designing the Medical Towers, Kahn started with the two main tenets of modern architecture: a clear response to program and an honest expression of materials. He investigated how scientists work in a laboratory and found that flexible areas away from direct light were best. These he surrounded with areas next to windows where the scientists could go to the light to work on their notes. These two areas, combined into one space, became a unit that was structurally supported with pre-cast, post-tensioned concrete, and was "served" by great towers that contained stairs and ducts for ventilation. Three of these spaces with their service towers were then clustered around a main service core, and the arrangement was multiplied vertically seven times to make a seven story building. (Two additional sections known as the Biology Building were subsequently added to complete the complex.)

In attempting to work within the means and ends of modern architecture, Kahn began to find both inadequate. In looking at the program of the spaces for the building, he found it necessary to go beyond merely listing the functions and the spaces. He distinguished a hierarchy of spaces, and made what he called "served" and "servant" spaces, the served spaces being for people and the servant spaces for pipes and ducts. This hierarchical differentiation began a more intense exploration of experience than had been present in modern architecture. Similarly, Kahn started his investigation of materials within the limits of modern architecture, but soon found these limits too confining. Because of developing technology, materials and their applications are continually changing. At the time the Medical Towers were built, red brick had not been used in an important modern building for over twenty years. When Kahn chose red brick, there was no recent tradition to rely on, and he found a rational analysis of brick's properties inadequate. It was at this point that he began developing his "conversation with the brick" as a means of finding its nature in its beginnings. Once its nature was known, its proper use could follow.

Kahn could have challenged modern architecture by denying it, by turning against rationalism and functionalism. But he did something different. He challenged modern architecture by entering fully into it and coming out the other side. He pushed rationalism to its limits, and when he needed more than rationalism would give, he moved on to a deeper analysis of what he called Order.

View of the laboratories across the
pond, as seen from the botanical
gardens at the rear of the complex.

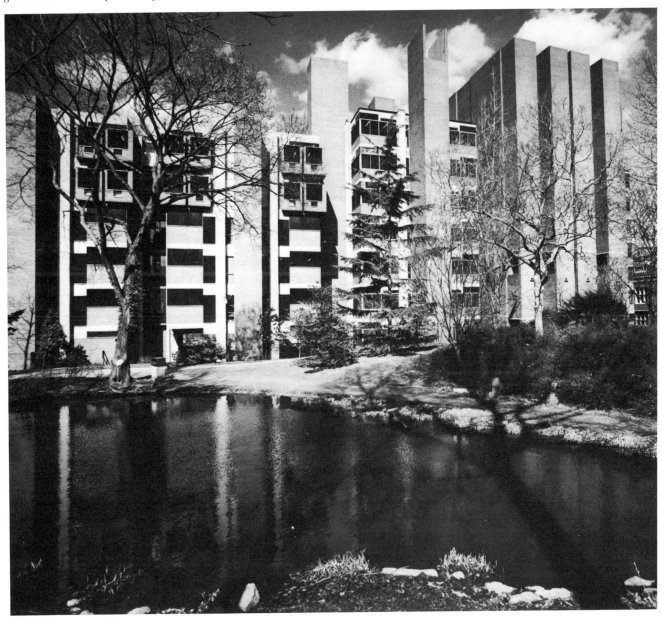

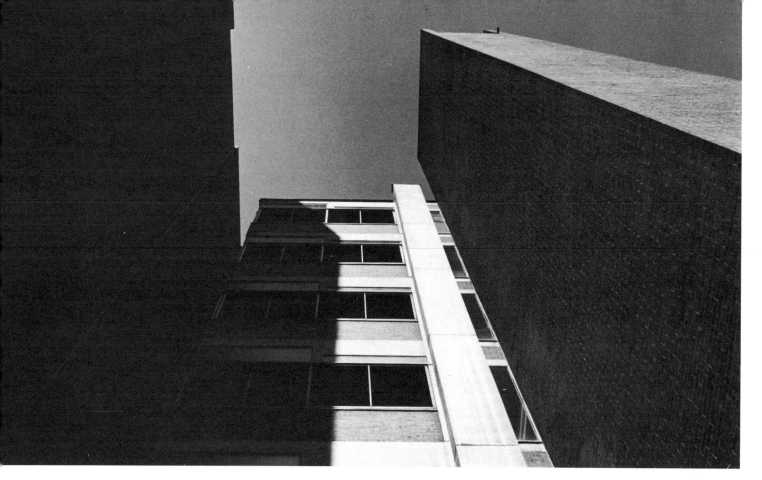

At the center are the laboratory floors.
To the right is a stair tower. To the left
is the main service core of the building.

Entrance to the biology building. The
concrete columns and cantilevered
beams are precast.

View from entrance at north side.

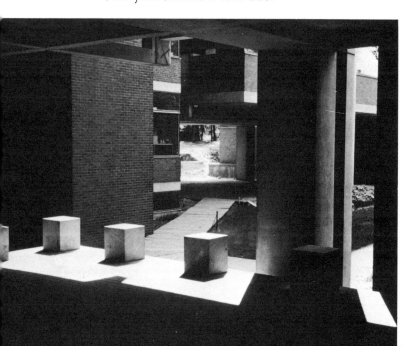

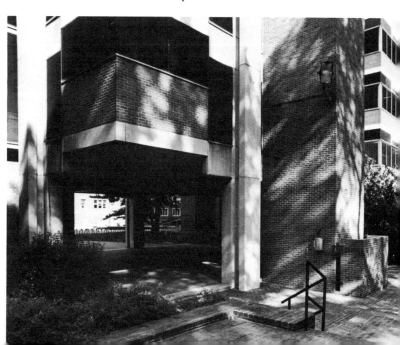

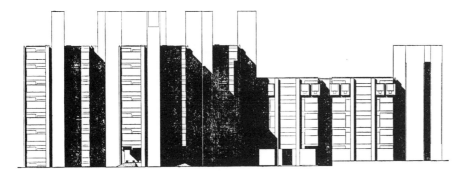

Elevation

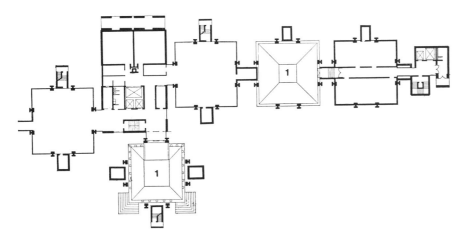

Ground-floor plan

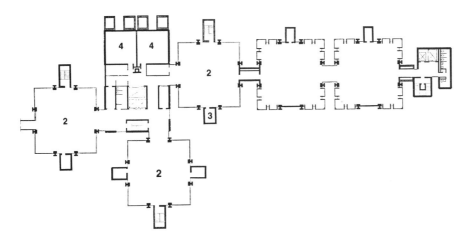

Typical floor plan

1 Entrance
2 Laboratory
3 Air duct tower
4 Storage

Salk Institute for Biological Studies

10010 North Torrey Pines Road
La Jolla, California

1959-65

The Medical Towers had certain functional limitations. Laboratory spaces were too small, exposed ducts in the ceilings accumulated dust, and unshaded light coming through the windows was disruptive to the scientists. In the laboratory buildings for the Salk Institute, Kahn overcame these limitations. The laboratory spaces were made larger and more flexible, the ducts were given a closed space of their own, and great overhangs protected the windows from direct sunlight. There are, however, more important differences between the Medical Towers and the Salk Institute. The Salk Institute was Kahn's first complete vision of a new architecture, one which responds to the whole human being. Kahn said [24]:

> When Salk came to my office and asked me to build a laboratory he said, "There is one thing which I would like to be able to accomplish. I would like to invite Picasso to the laboratory." He was implying, of course, that in science, concerned with measurement, there is this will of the least living thing to be itself. The microbe wants to be a microbe, the rose wants to be a rose, and man wants to be man, to express. This desire to express was sensed by Salk: that the scientist needed the presence of the unmeasurable, which is the realm of the artist.

Kahn designed the Salk Institute as a mandala. In Oriental art, the mandala represents natural order and hierarchy through the use of a series of concentric geometric shapes, each containing an image of a deity or an attribute of a deity. In Jungian psychology, the mandala is seen as a means of reunifying the various aspects of the self. Kahn's building radiates inward from the exterior utility spaces containing stairs and toilets (body); through the laboratory spaces—where the biological research takes place—which are hermetically sealed, monitored by computer, and served by great spaces for ducts and equipment (mind); through the walkways, which are places of meeting (society); through the private teak screened offices of the scientists with their ocean views, which are places of contemplation; to the central court with a simple band of water running through it, which is a place of stillness, a facade to the sky, a roofless cathedral (spirit). Thus, the progression is body, mind, society, spirit: the attributes of the whole human being. A great building must serve each of these well and be a means for integrating them.

In the Salk Institute Kahn recaptured the richness of the forms and materials of the great historical architectures, and arranged those forms and materials between earth and sky so as to communicate to us things about ourselves we would otherwise not know. Modern architecture had become fascinated by the machine-like quality of the glass box. Kahn, in designing a laboratory, also used glass to encase the work spaces, but he then wrapped the glass in concrete, in the rich forms of history. Then, between the two wings of the building, he opened a central courtyard, a place of stillness, of Silence.

View down the axis of the court with a band of water pointing toward the ocean in the distance. On either side are towers with the offices, or studies, of the scientists, their walls angled toward the ocean.

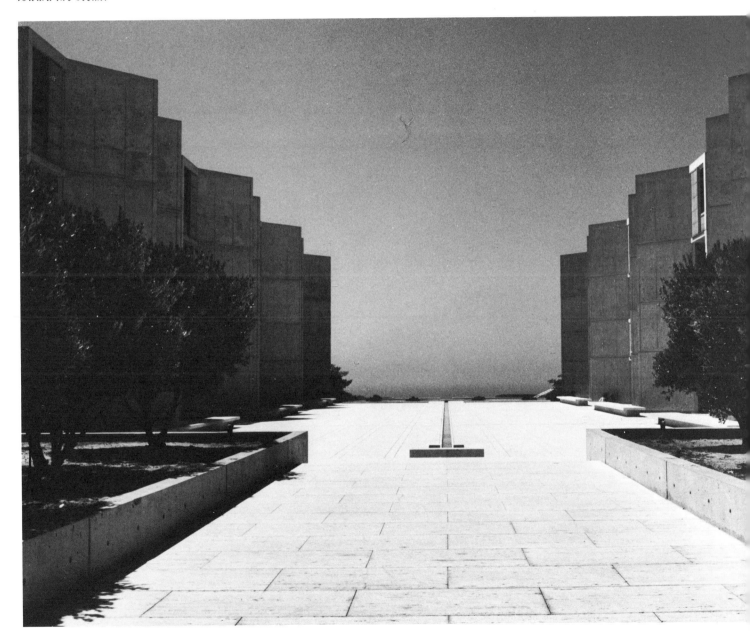

The laboratory complex as seen from cliffs near the ocean.

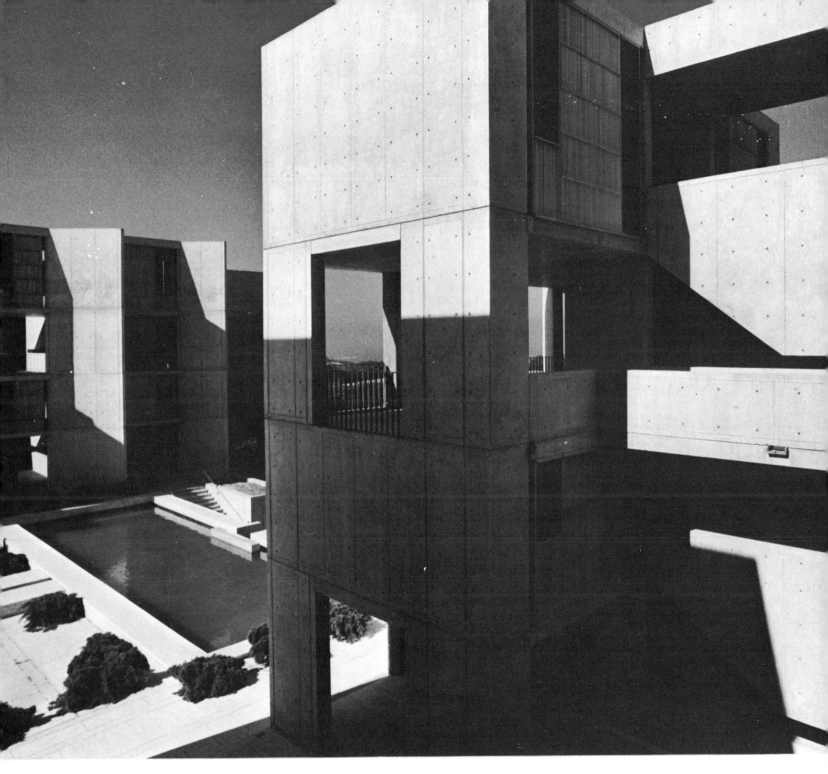

*Standing on a walkway in front of
a laboratory and looking out toward a
tower with four studies. Beyond the
fountain pool in the court is another
study tower.*

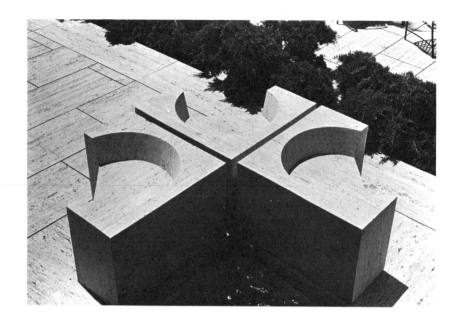

At the base of the fountain are large sculptural forms cut in travertine.

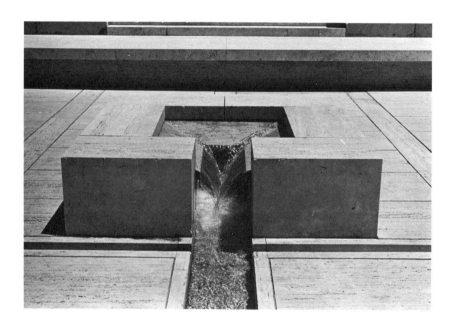

Near the entrance to the court is the source for the band of water that runs down the court and becomes the fountain at the other end.

A view of the studies showing the sliding teak screens that protect the studies from the sun.

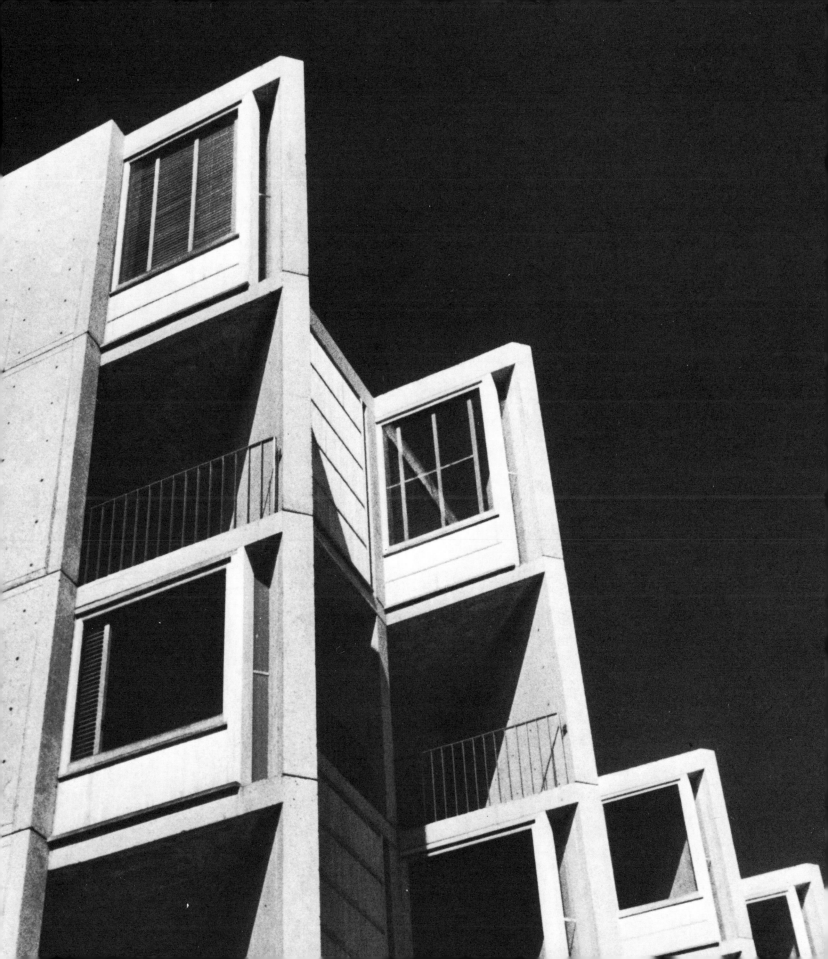

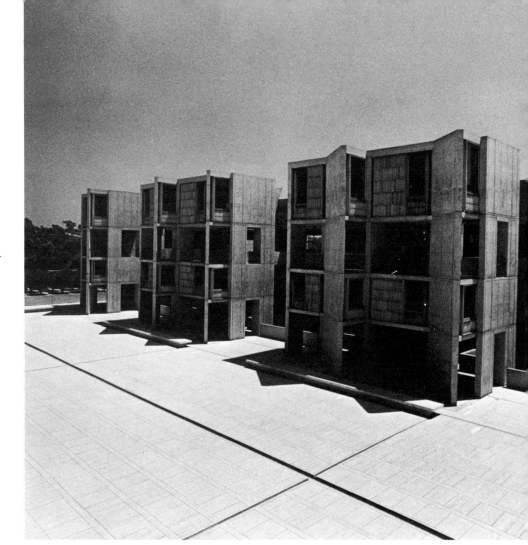

View from an upper walkway. The buildings are made of exposed concrete. The court is paved with travertine. Between the study towers on the other side of the court can be seen the alternating laboratory and service floors.

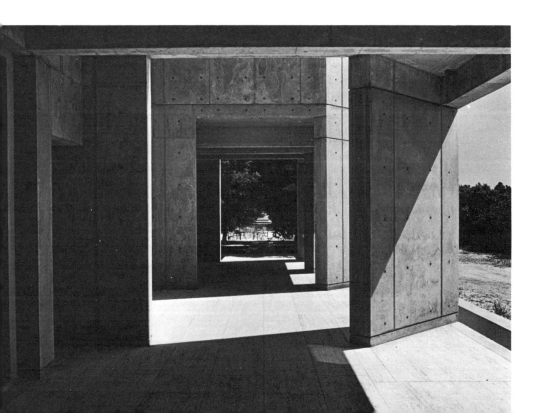

Walkway under the library.

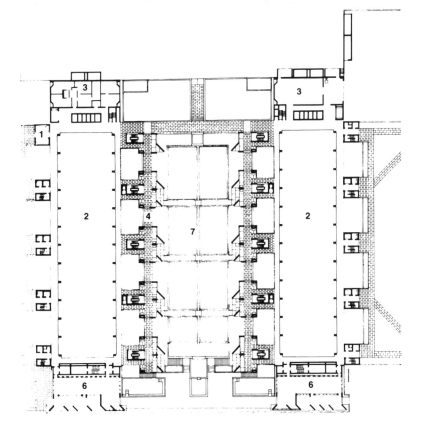

Plan

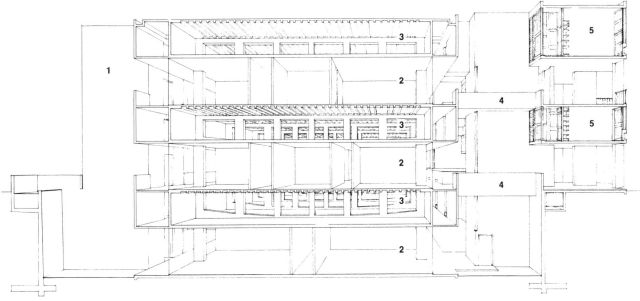

Section

1 Stair and toilet tower
2 Laboratory
3 Mechanical equipment
4 Walkway
5 Study
6 Library
7 Courtyard

Salk Institute Community Center
(THE SALK MEETING HOUSE)

La Jolla, California
1959-65 (project, not built)

The Salk Institute was planned to be a complex of
three parts: the laboratories, which were built, and resi-
dences and a meeting house, neither of which was
built because of financial limitations. The Meeting
House, although it exists only in drawings, is one of
Kahn's great achievements. It is a series of rooms and an
auditorium surrounding a great enclosed interior court
that has no designated function. It might be used for
formal dinners or meetings, but its character lies in not
having a designated use. It is a fertile potential, a place
for things which are not yet, which still "desire to be."

    The shapes that Kahn used in the Meeting House
and the strong geometry that organizes these shapes de-
rive in part from ancient Roman architecture. With
these references, Kahn showed how modern architects
could learn from the organizing principles of the past,
and in so doing, once again open up architecture to
history. Kahn used some of these shapes, specifically the
square enclosed in a circle and the circle enclosed in
a square, to give some of the rooms double walls. In
Kahn's design the sun comes through openings in the
outer wall and is reflected back and forth between the
two walls before entering the room. Thus, he was
able to modulate and sculpt the incoming light with the
thin walls of modern architecture rather than the massive walls used by the ancient architects.

    Several of Kahn's projects were never built. He
said [19]:

> That which is not built is not really lost. Once its
> value is established, its demand for presence is undeni-
> able. It is merely waiting for the right circumstances.

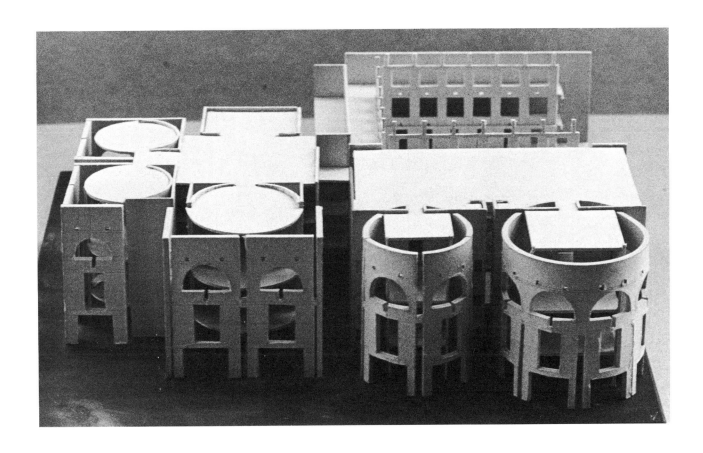

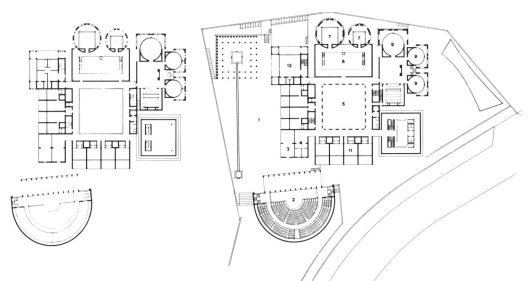

Second-floor plan	**First-floor plan**

1 Garden
2 Auditorium
3 Entrance porch
4 Entrance
5 Banquet hall
6 Library
7 Reading-room
8 Kitchen
9 Dining
10 Gymnasium
11 Guest
12 Director's quarters

Sher-E-Bangla-Nagar, Master Plan

(CAPITAL COMPLEX PLAN)

Dacca, Bangladesh
1962 — (not completed)

Kahn loved the city. He thought of the city as the place of gathering for human institutions, and he thought of the arrangements of streets and buildings as a talking to each other by the institutions. In his Sher-E-Bangla-Nagar Master Plan, originally the plan for the Second Capital of Pakistan, he sought the right relationships among the Assembly, the Mosque, and the Supreme Court. He said [16]:

"I was given an extensive program of buildings: the Assembly, the Supreme Court, hostels, schools, a stadium, the diplomatic enclave, the living sector, a market, all to be placed on a thousand acres of flat land subject to flood. I kept thinking of how these buildings might be grouped, and what would cause them to take their place on the land. On the night of the third day, I fell out of bed with a thought that is still the prevailing idea of the plan. This came simply from the realization that assembly is of a transcendent nature. Men came to assemble to touch the spirit of community, and I felt that this must be expressible. Observing the way of religion in the life of the Pakistani, I thought that a mosque woven into the space fabric of the assembly would reflect this feeling.

"In my mind the Supreme Court was the test of the acts of legislation against the philosophic view of the nature of man. The three [the Assembly, the Mosque, and the Supreme Court] became inseparable in thinking of the transcendent nature of assembly.

"It was presumptuous to assume this was right. How did I know that it would fit their way of life. But this assumption took possession.

"We saw the Chief Justice the next day, and we were greeted with the usual tea and biscuits. He said: 'I know why you're here—the grapevine is very well developed in Pakistan. You're barking up the wrong tree, because I will not be a part of this assembly group. I will go to the provincial capital site near the provincial high court where the lawyers are, and I think I will feel much more at home there.' I turned to him and said, 'Mr. Chief Justice, is this your decision alone or is it also the decision of the judges who will follow you? Let me explain to you what I intend to compose.' And I made my first sketch on paper of the Assembly with the Mosque on the lake. I added the hostels framing this lake. I told him how I felt about the transcendent meaning of assembly. After a moment's thought he took the pencil out of my hand and placed a mark representing the Supreme Court in a position where I would have placed it myself, on the other side of the Mosque, and he said: 'The Mosque is sufficient insulation from the men of the Assembly.' "

In describing the complex, Kahn said [24]:

"My design at Dacca is inspired, actually, by the Baths of Caracalla [the great Roman public baths], but much extended. The residential spaces of this building are an amphitheater. This is residual space, a space that is found, a court. Around it there are gardens, and in the body of the building, which is the amphitheater, are the interiors, and in the interiors are levels of gardens and places that honor the athlete and places that honor the knowledge of how you were made. All these are places of well-being and places for rest and places where one gets advice about how to live forever . . . and so that is what inspired the design."

Model of the Master Plan (late version).

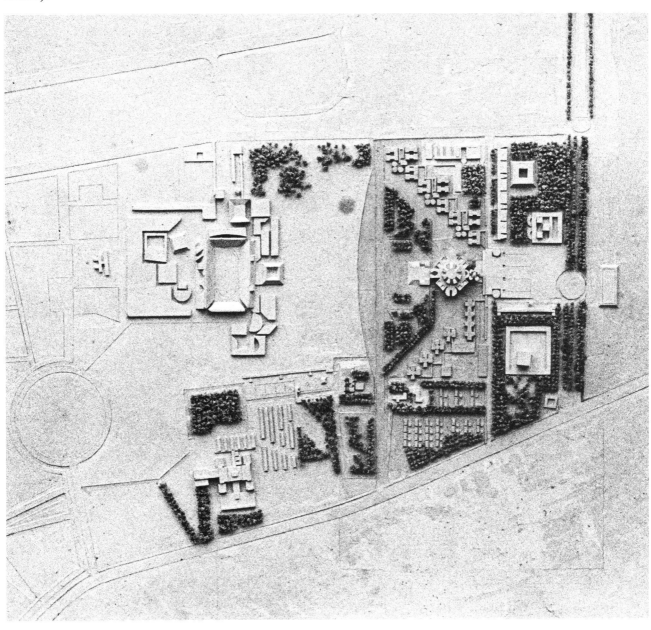

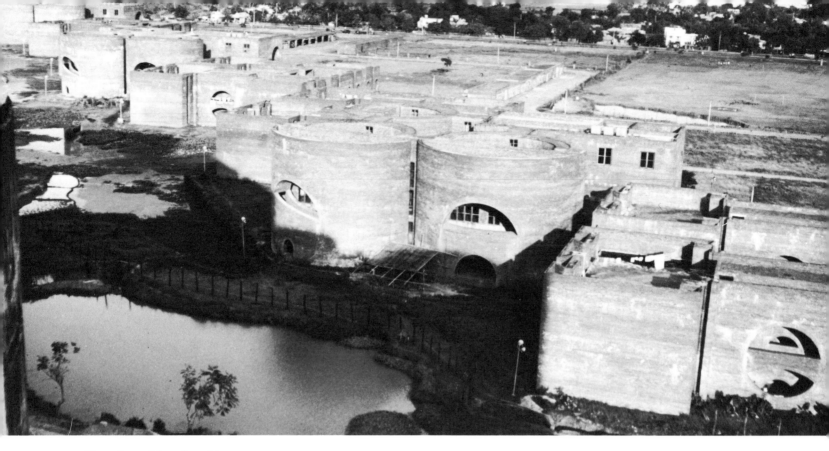

Two views of hostels and lounge
buildings used by members of the
National Assembly.

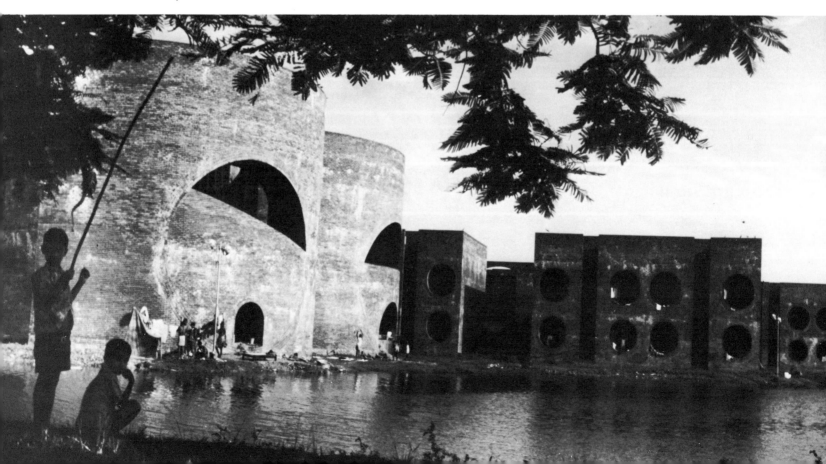

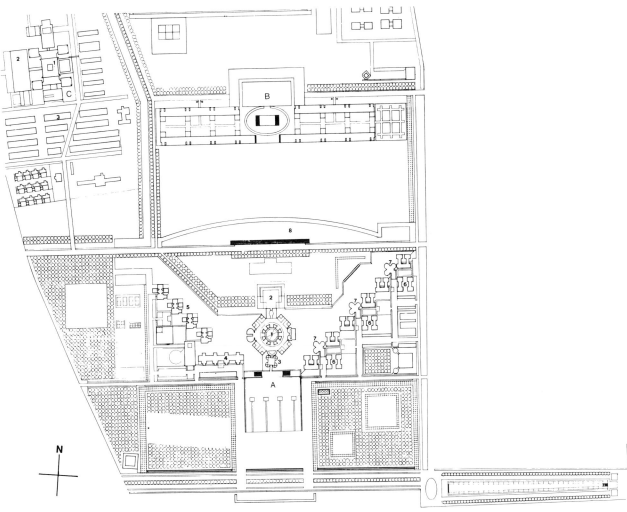

Plan

A Citadel of the Assembly
1 Assembly building
2 Presidential Square
3 Prayer Hall
4 Hostels for Ministers
5 Hostels for Secretaries
6 Hostels for members of the Assembly

7 Dining halls
8 Lake
B Secretariat
C Hospital complex
1 Hospital
2 Out-Patient department
3 Staff housing

National Assembly Hall, Sher-E-Bangla-Nagar

Dacca, Bangladesh

1962 — (not completed)

The National Assembly Hall for the capital complex in Dacca is one of a series of projects in which Kahn rediscovered the center of the building as a primary ordering force. In speaking of the building Kahn said [17]:

> The Assembly is a place of transcendence for political people. In a house of legislation, you are dealing with circumstantial conditions. The assembly establishes or modifies the institutions of man. So I could see the thing right from the start as the citadel of assembly and the citadel of the institutions of man, which were opposite, and I symbolized the institutions of man. I made the entrance to the Assembly a Mosque. I was setting the nature of it, because I noticed that the people prayed five times a day. In the program there was a note which said that there should be a prayer room of 3,000 square feet, and a closet to hold rugs; that was the program. I made them a Mosque which was 30,000 square feet, and the prayer rugs were always on the floor. And that became the entrance, that is to say, the Mosque became the entrance. When I presented this to the authorities, they accepted it right away.

A great hall is at the center of this building and is lit by natural light from above. The roof over the hall becomes a giant structure for transforming the light as it shines in through holes of various shapes and reflects off of the great beams before coming down into the space.

Kahn's belief in the importance of a building's relationship to its institution can be seen in this statement [16]:

> What I am trying to do is establish, out of a philosophy, a *belief* that I can turn over to Pakistan, now Bangladesh, so that whatever they do is always answerable to it. I feel as though this plan, which was made weeks after I saw the program, has strength. Does it have all the ingredients? If only one is lacking, it will disintegrate.

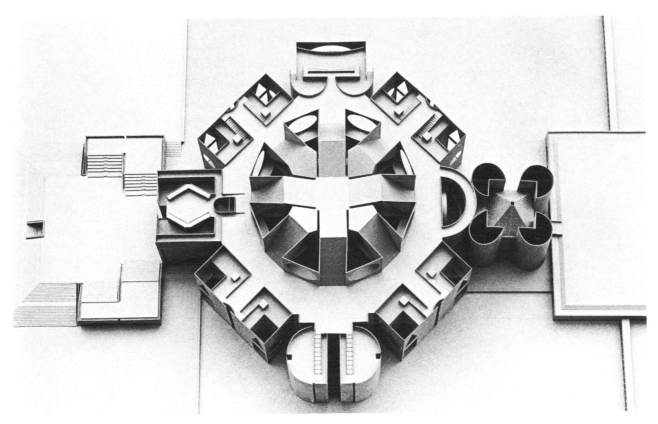

Model.

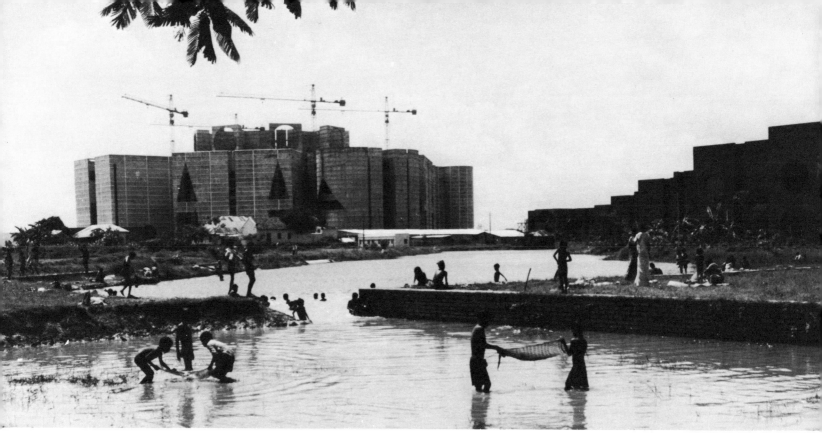

The National Assembly Hall seen from the Northwest. Cranes above the building are being used in construction.

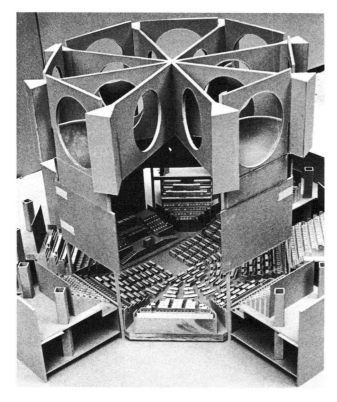

Cutaway model showing the interior of the Assembly chamber. The large holes in the roof structure are for bringing in light from above.

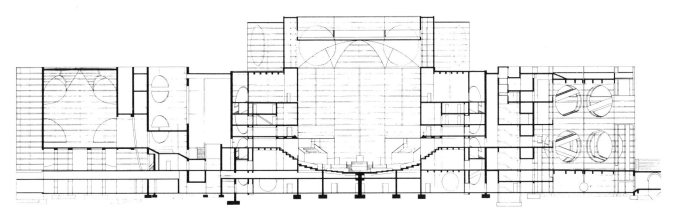

Section

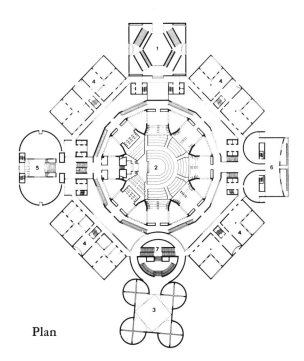

Plan

1 Entrance hall
2 Assembly Chamber
3 Prayer Hall
4 Offices
5 Ministers' lounge
6 Dining and recreation
7 Ablution Court

Kimbell Art Museum

Will Rogers Road West
Fort Worth, Texas

1966-72

The Kimbell Art Museum is Kahn's offering to Light. The materials are luminous, truly light that has spent itself, and the form of the building is dedicated to bringing the viewer and the paintings together in natural light. Most museums use artificial light because the ultraviolet in sunlight can damage paintings. However, Kahn preferred natural light, as it is alive and ever-changing. To deal with its damaging qualities, he brought it in through long skylights in the vaulted ceiling, and then used a screen inside to filter the light and reflect it off of the concrete ceiling. The exposed concrete of the ceiling, usually a dull material, here has a warm glow.

The building is simple and austere and at the same time rich and noble. Its richness comes, not from decoration applied as an afterthought, but rather from the reverence with which Kahn treats each of the materials. The structure is concrete, alive in the light; the walls are travertine, a form of limestone, here used as a non-structural surface material; the floors are oak, warm under foot; and the roof is lead, an ancient and impervious material that easily bends to fit the roof's curves, and which reflects a dull sheen in the southwestern sun.

View showing the vault-like forms of the roof, which are actually cycloids. The first one is open, making an outside porch. At the top of the others are skylights. The structural frame is concrete, the infill walls are travertine, and the roofs are lead.

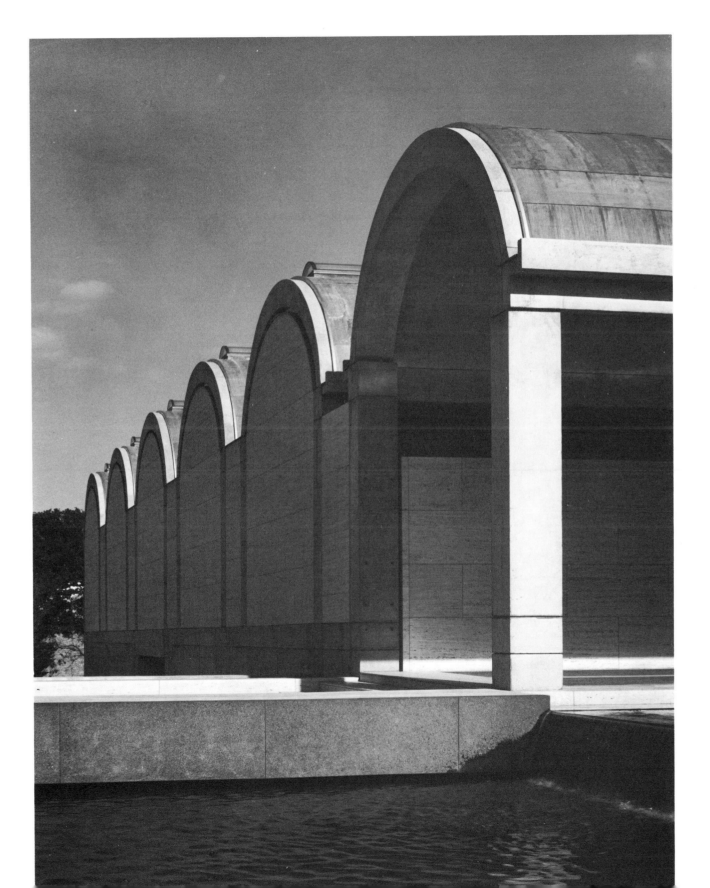

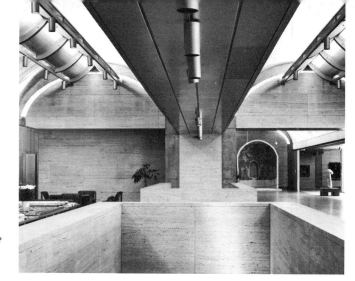

The low walls in the foreground are for stairs coming up to the galleries from the entrance level. Directly above is space for air conditioning ducts. To either side are the sky-lit cycloids.

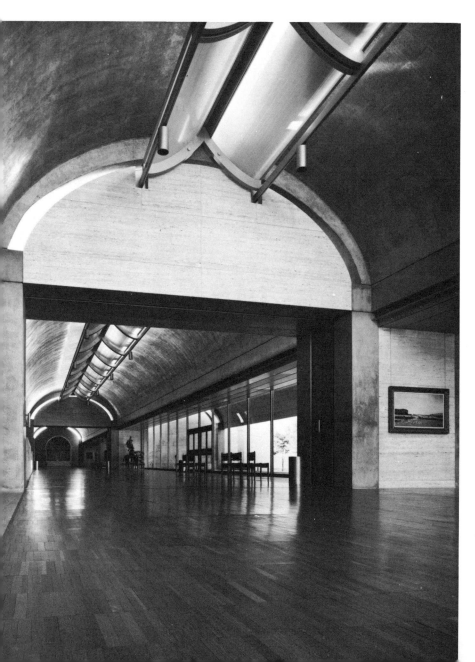

View down several sections of the ceiling. In the center of the cycloids are reflectors that hang under the skylights to reflect light back onto the curved concrete ceiling, giving it a warm glow. At the far end of the gallery is a medieval apse, part of the museum collection. To the right is the entrance from the park.

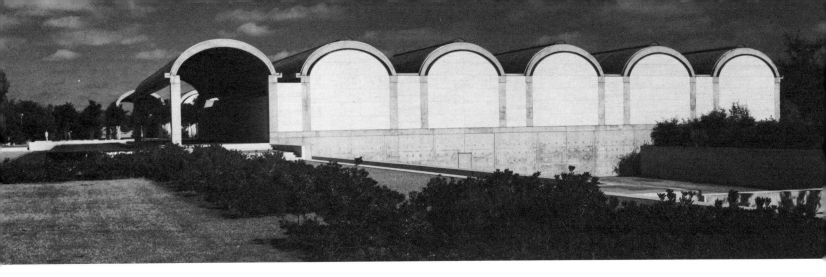

*View from the South showing west
entrance from the park.*

*Looking from the gallery into the
north court. The overhead wires form
a trellis for vines, which will provide
shade from the sun.*

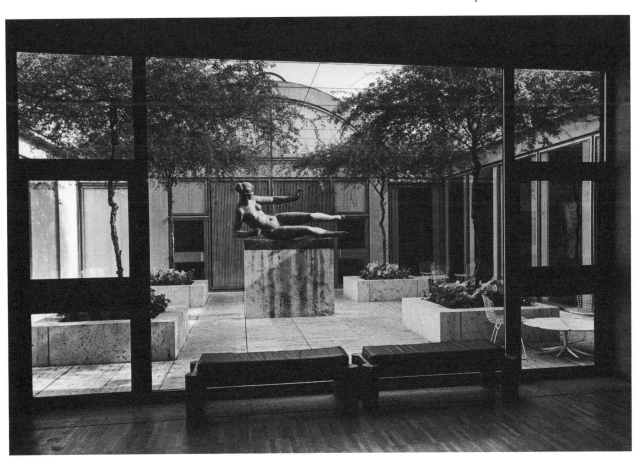

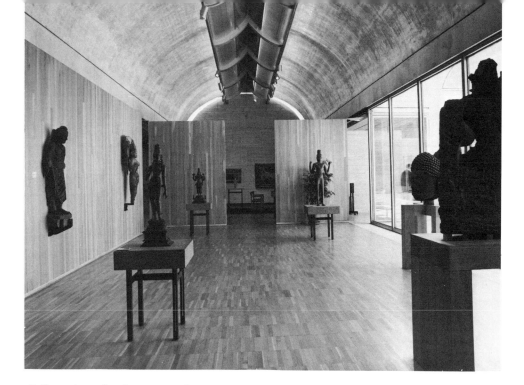

Gallery views showing system of movable partitions for displaying paintings.

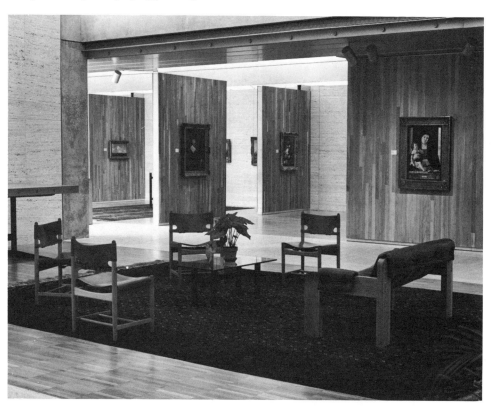

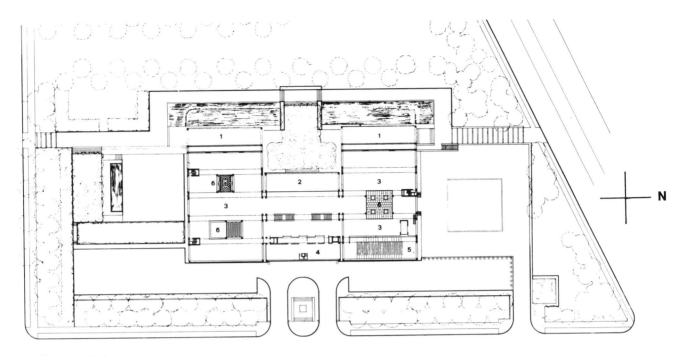

Gallery-level plan

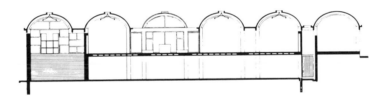

Section

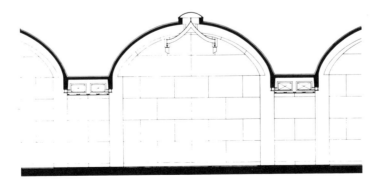

Section showing one of the cycloids

1 Porch
2 Entrance
3 Gallery
4 Library
5 Auditorium
6 Open court

Library, Phillips Exeter Academy

Exeter, New Hampshire

1967-72

For the Exeter Library, Kahn again used a great central space. In classical and neoclassical buildings, the central space had symbolized a social hierarchy, with certain people or functions occupying the center and others relegated to the periphery. Modern architecture had rejected this centrality as undemocratic. Frank Lloyd Wright placed a massive fireplace at the center of his early houses, displacing people from the center to move about it in an architectural version of the Copernican revolution. The European architects, such as Le Corbusier, used a grid made up of columns that made all of the spaces equally important and none central.

But Kahn realized that hierarchy is not necessarily incompatible with democratic ideals. The differences among people implied by previous hierarchies can be internalized into each person. Kahn's realization was similar to those of Freud and Jung, who saw the great human dramas, which had previously been acted out by Oedipus, the Hero, or the Mother Goddess, internalized into the individual's psyche. By reflecting a full range of human complexity, or hierarchy, in his buildings, Kahn restored a richness to architecture that had to a large extent been absent in the modern movement.

In the Exeter Library, Kahn was concerned with how the person and the book come together. He said [19]:

> I see the library as a place where the librarian can lay out the books, open especially to selected pages to seduce the reader. There should be a place with great tables on which the librarian can put the books, and the reader should be able to take the book and go to the light.

At Exeter, Kahn designed a great central space. Through the roof, through the stacks, and through the great circular shapes cut in the walls, light comes into the space. In this central space, the librarian can display books, and the reader can then carry them to study carrels, or alcoves, along the perimeter of the building.

The carrels are illuminated by great windows starting above the eye level of the reader, and each carrel has a smaller eye-level window with a sliding wooden shutter, which can be closed for privacy and concentration, or opened to permit a view of the wooded campus.

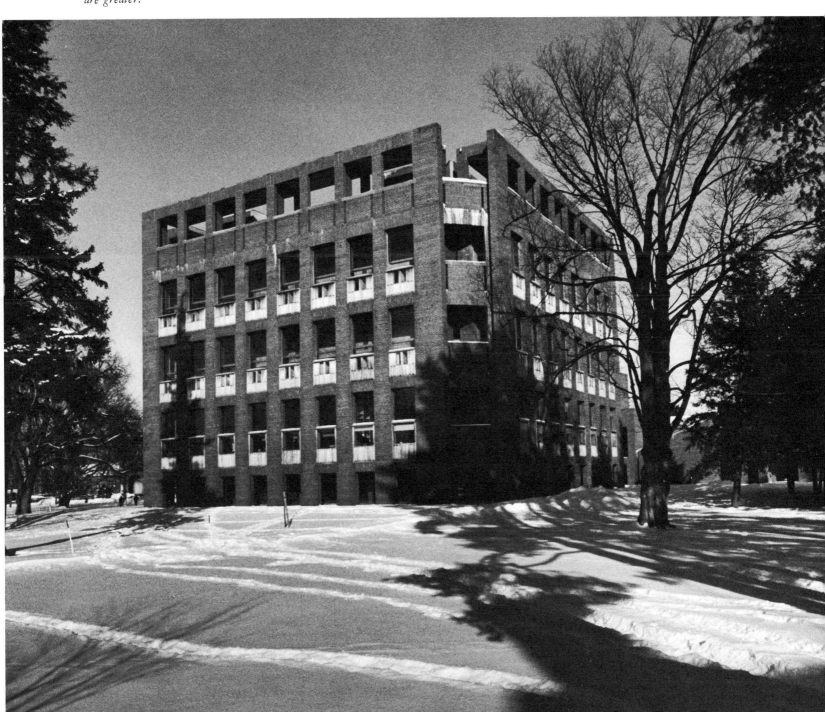

Overall view. The building exterior
is brick in keeping with the traditional
New England campus. The brick piers
between the windows become wider
nearer to the ground where their loads
are greater.

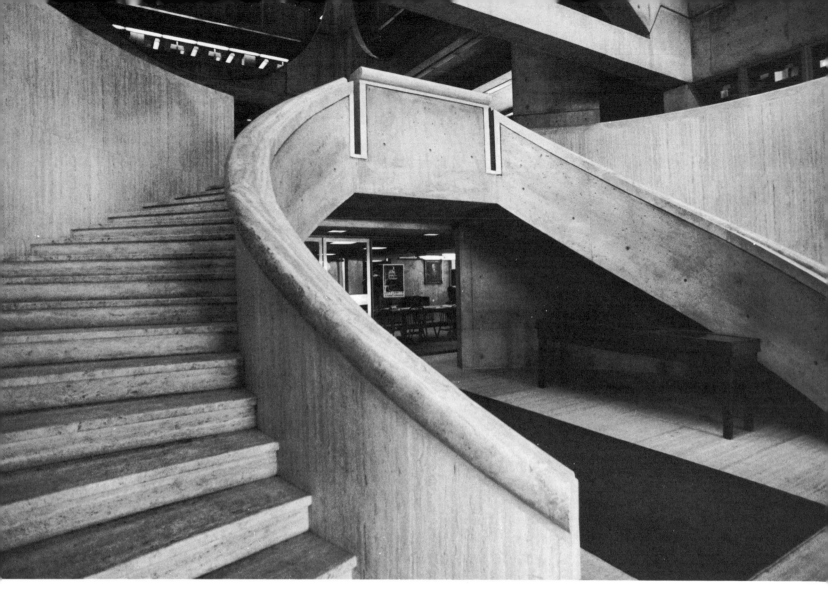

Main stair up from entrance level to
the central hall. The massive banister is
concrete and is surfaced with travertine
where people come into contact with it.

The central hall. Beyond the great
circles are balconies containing the
book stacks. The crossed beams at the
top support the roof and also reflect the
light from windows under the roof.

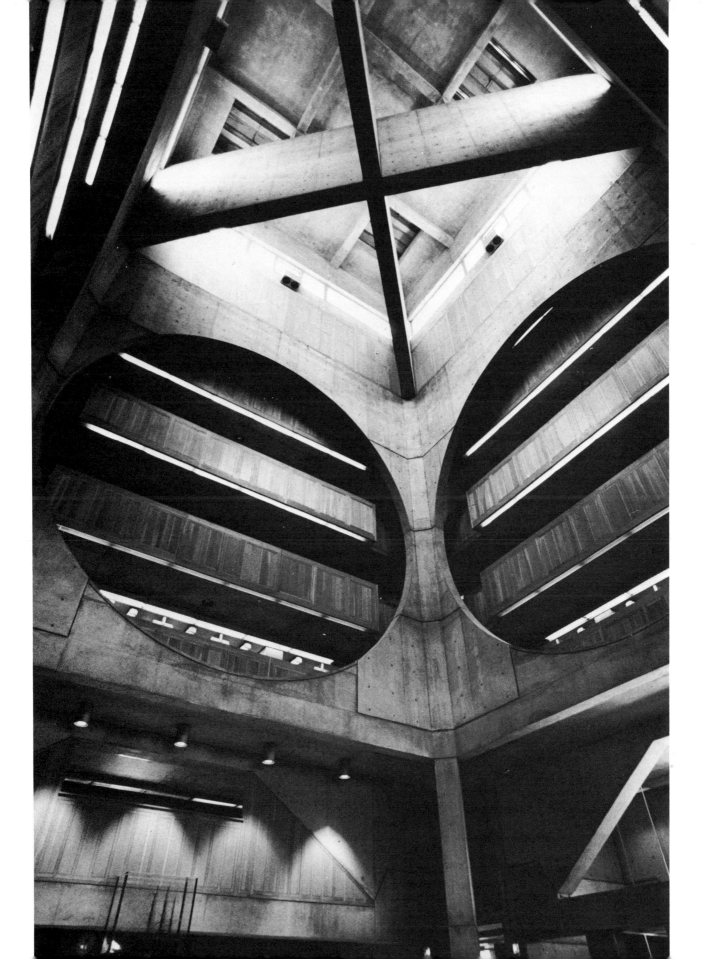

Individual study carrels, or alcoves, along the perimeter of the building. A sliding wood shutter permits the closing of the small window at eye level. Wood is used for the carrels and in other places where people are in physical contact with the building.

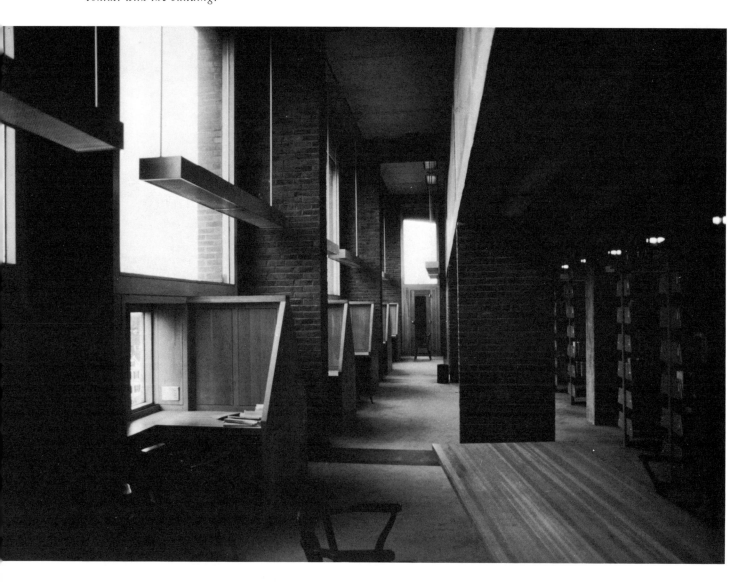

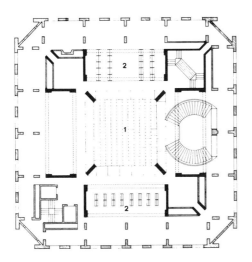

Entrance floor plan

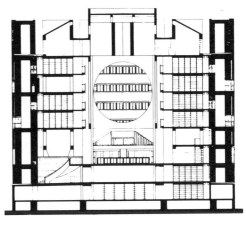

Section

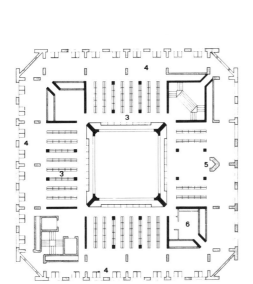

Third-floor plan

1 Central hall
2 Reference and periodicals
3 Books
4 Carrels
5 Fireplace
6 Toilets

Yale Center for British Art and Studies

1080 Chapel Street
New Haven, Connecticut

1969-74

Finished after his death, the British Center embodies
many of Kahn's concerns. The building is urban in
character, with shops along the street on the ground
floor. It is clad in grey, pewter-colored stainless steel.
Here again, Kahn was designing on the edge of available
technology, using a new steel finish for the first time.
This finish gives the steel the quality of slate, dark and
grey in the climate of this old New England town.

   Dark on the outside, the building explodes with
light inside. A system of skylights brings ultraviolet-free
light into the galleries of the top floor and, in two courts,
brings this light down into the building. The courts
are paneled in a luminous light oak and have balconies
looking into them from the other floors of the building.
One court is at the entrance. The other is near the center
of the building and is Kahn's last offering to Silence,
a space without a function, a place for that which is
not yet.

*View from the Northeast. The near
corner is the entrance, and to the right
are shops at the ground level. The walls
are paneled with specially finished
stainless steel. The skylights are just
visible at the roofline.*

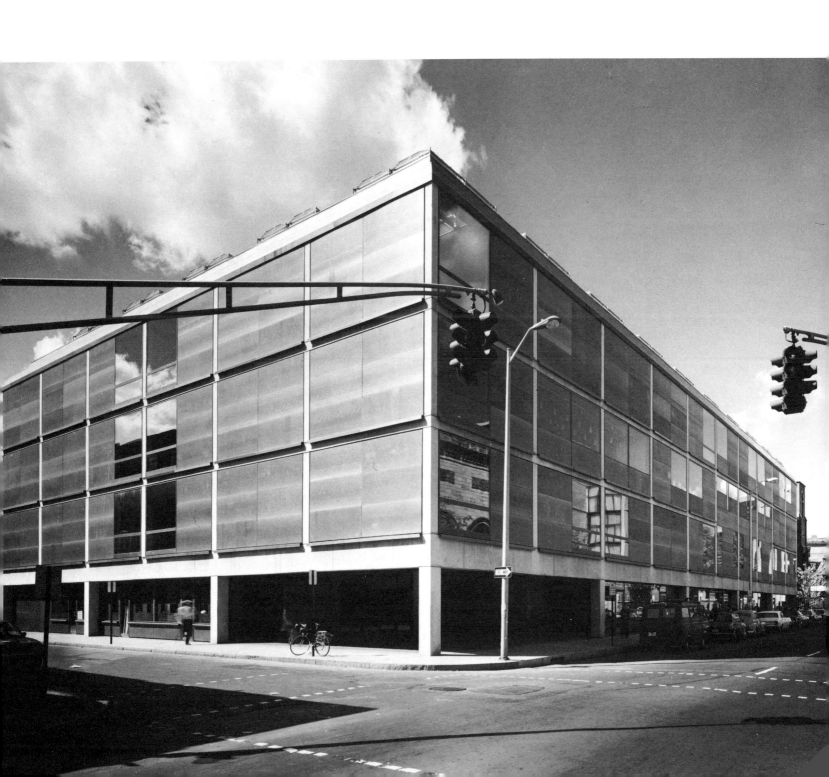

The main court. In the foreground to the right is the round form of the stair tower.

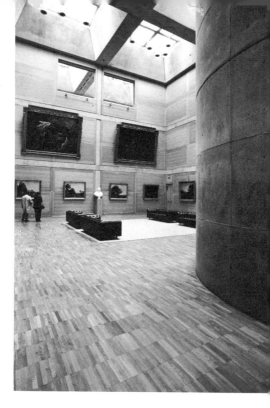

Galleries on the upper floor. At the center is a view into the entrance court. The partitions to the left are movable.

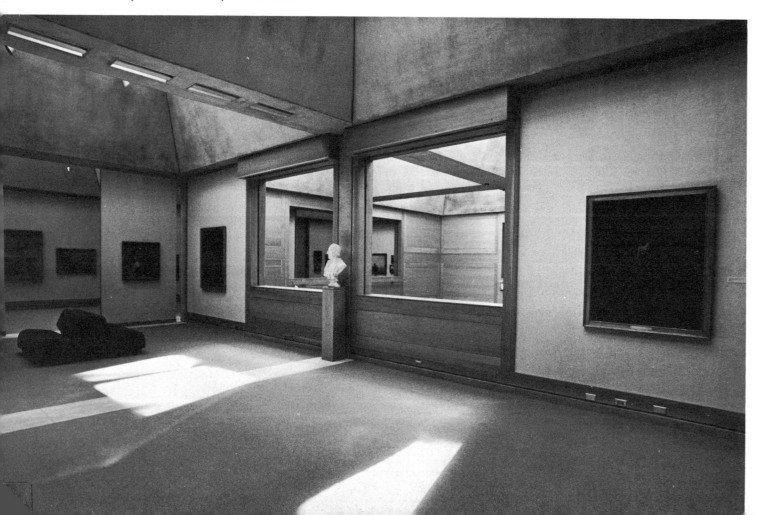

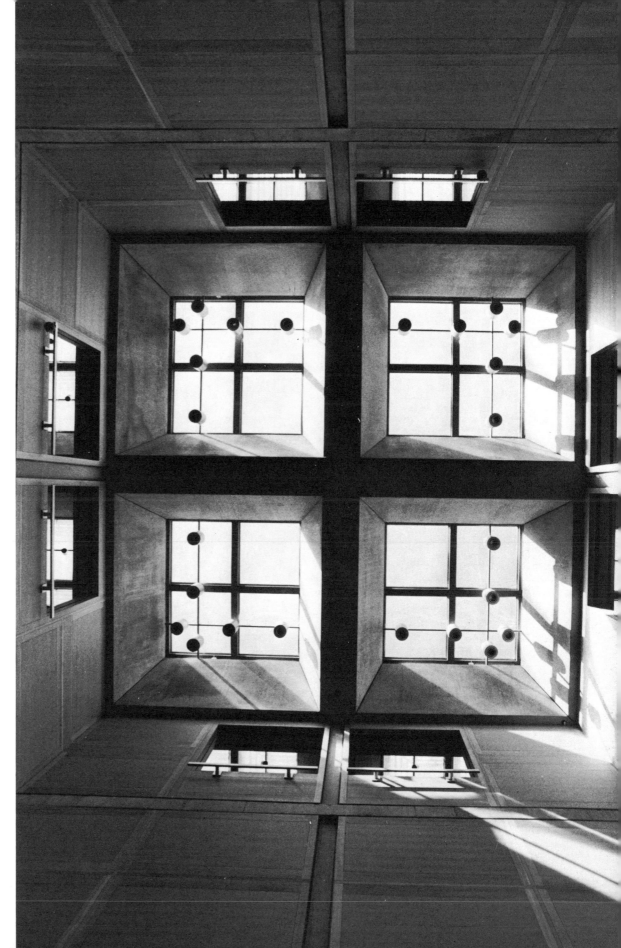

*Skylights over
the entrance court.*

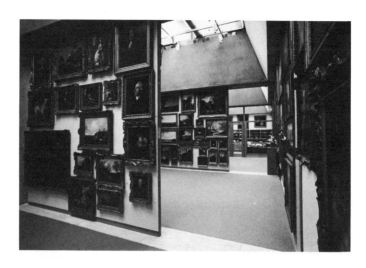

Special study gallery.

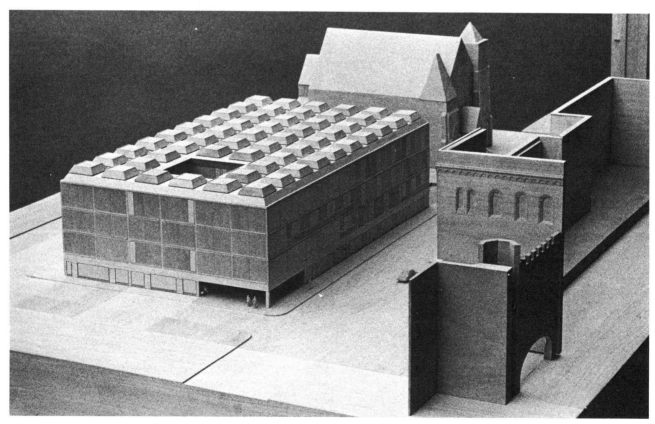

Model.

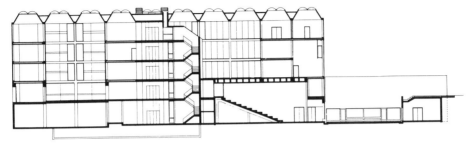

Section

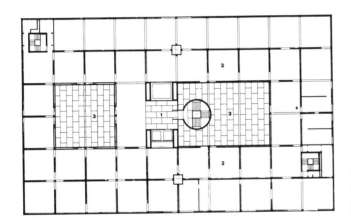

1 Lobby
2 Gallery
3 Light Court

Fourth-floor plan

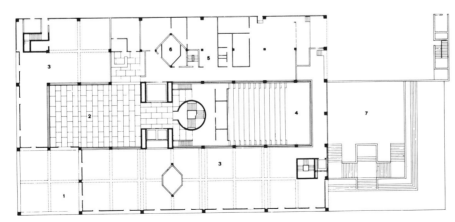

1 Entrance porch
2 Court
3 Shops
4 Auditorium
5 Service
6 Air duct
7 Lower court and shops

Street-level plan

Appendices

Biographical Note on Louis I. Kahn

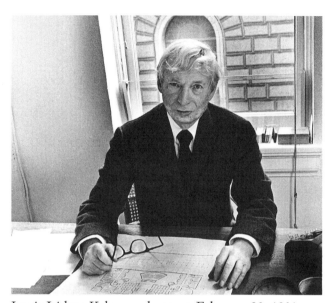

Louis Isidore Kahn was born on February 20, 1901, on the Baltic island of Saarama, Estonia (Russia). There, as a young boy, his face was scarred by fire while carrying hot coals. He emigrated with his parents to Philadelphia in 1905, where they lived in poverty. His upbringing was a traditional Jewish one, although not strictly Orthodox, and his later pursuit of knowledge always had a Talmudic, questioning quality to it. As a high school student, Kahn was gifted as a painter and a musician, winning citywide art prizes and supporting his family by playing the piano in silent movie theaters. He had won a scholarship to study art, but in his last year of high school he took a course in architectural history and resolved to become an architect.

From 1920 to 1924, he studied architecture at the University of Pennsylvania, earning his tuition as a teaching assistant. The University of Pennsylvania was at that time a school in the Beaux-Arts tradition under the leadership of the respected architect and teacher, Paul Philippe Cret. Kahn was an exceptional student, and after graduating, he worked in important architec-tural offices. He also traveled to see historic European architecture and, during the depression, organized a research group composed of unemployed architects and engineers. Kahn's Beaux-Arts training made it difficult for him to come to terms with the modern movement in architecture, and although he became an outspoken thinker and theorist, his early buildings were undistinguished.

From 1947 until 1957, Kahn taught architecture at Yale. He had acquired a reputation as a thinker rather than a doer until 1951-53, when he designed the Yale University Art Gallery, which contained the seeds of his later ideas. Then, in 1957-61, he designed the Richards Medical Research Building in Philadelphia, and it was quickly recognized as a major contribution to modern architecture. Kahn's maturation in his late fifties was exceptional, even in the field of architecture, which tends to be a late-maturing field and tends to see long-lived practices with significant work done late in life. From 1957 until his death in 1974, Kahn taught at the University of Pennsylvania. For many of those years, his studio was in a beautiful vaulted space in the top of an old library. Twice a week he and his fellow critics would meet with students from all over the world; the classes became known for lively and profound discussions that often continued late into the night, sometimes adjourning to a nearby restaurant or apartment.

Kahn was the intellectual and spiritual leader of the school at the time of its rebirth, when it again became the finest architecture school in the country, a position it had held when Kahn was a student there. The school was also at the center of the rejuvenation of the city of Philadelphia and the emergence of a new architecture in this country.

Through his sixties and into his seventies, Kahn designed buildings and projects in several countries for the major human institutions: residence, religion, art, government, science, industry, theater, and education.

His buildings were great contributions to architecture and to human culture, and several in this country are ranked among our finest. He gained recognition as one of the leading modern architects and was awarded gold medals and honorary degrees, among these, the Gold Medal from the American Institute of Architects, and the Royal Gold Medal for Architecture from the Royal Institute of British Architects. He was also made a Fellow of the American Academy of Arts and Letters. Many of his contemporaries felt fortunate to be influenced by a person they believed to be one of the most powerful architectural minds of all times, one that encompassed the deepest meaning and spirit of architecture.

Although Kahn was absorbed in his architectural practice and was fortunate to complete many commissions, his circumstances were at times miserable. His method of working, which was frequently slow, excluded him from commissions by clients who were motivated by expediency or profit. Business inefficiency in Kahn's office and his commissions in India and Pakistan, which sometimes consumed great expenses and then fell through, burdened Kahn with crushing debts. What is remarkable is that he was able to practice architecture as the highest of arts—totally uncompromised by expediency—and not only to survive, but also to complete so many exceptional buildings.

Kahn died of a heart attack on March 17, 1974, alone in the men's room at Penn Station in New York. He was returning from a trip in India and had missed several connections trying to get back to Philadelphia for his classes. Despite his age of seventy-three, his death must be considered premature, as he was under extreme pressure from his finances, work that was going poorly, and the stress of traveling alone to and from India and Bangladesh twice in a short period of time. He was at the height of his creative powers and doing some of his finest work at the time of his death.

Due to the carelessness of New York authorities, his body lay unclaimed for two days after his death.

The following are some of the remarks made at memorials for Kahn in Philadelphia and New York [29]:

He was the most complete intellectual I'd ever known. I think this was because his intellect was so strong, that it was all through his body. His body knew what his mind knew, which I think is one reason why he was a great architect. . . . Nobody ever gave off so much light. It was a physical light that came from the activity of his imagination and the aliveness of his intellect through all his pores. . . .

—Vincent Scully

Kahn was working within the realization of the individual, his homecomings, his departure, his scale to place and to nature. . . . Few architects placed more attention on the subtle transition of human activity: from work to relaxation, to play, to comfort, with no separation or distinctions—but reaching for a simple dignity in the acts of life.

—Romaldo Giurgola

. . . The essential is not the disguise but the inflexible metal of creative will power.

—Robert Le Ricolais

Lou Kahn materially influences every architect, not merely through his visible works of architecture, but by the principles he enunciated so beautifully. . . .

—Norman Rice

Biographical Note on John Lobell

John Lobell has a wide-ranging mind addressing many areas besides architecture, including spiritual traditions, cultural theory, consciousness, mythology, Buddhism, information theory, and quantum theory. He is the author of several books and numerous articles, is a contributor to several websites, and has lectured and addressed conferences throughout the country.

He received his architecture degrees from the University of Pennsylvania, where Kahn taught, and where he studied with Edmund Bacon, Denise Scott Brown, Robert Geddes, Romaldo Giurgola, G. Holmes Perkins, and Robert Venturi among others. He is a professor of architecture at Pratt Institute in Brooklyn, New York.

Lobell has served on the board of the Architectural League of New York and on the advisory board of the Joseph Campbell Foundation, and he has worked in various architectural offices, including Harrison and Abramovitz, Abe Geller, and Ulrich Franzen, where he was project manager on an exploration of urban form funded by the Ford Foundation. He has also worked on several Internet and telecom projects and launched several companies.

Lobell is currently at work on a book looking at how Kahn's buildings manifest his spiritual philosophy, and a book on structures of consciousness, about which he says:

> We are now in the midst of the greatest scientific, technological, and therefore cultural changes in history, greater than those that brought about the modern era at the beginning to the twentieth century. Biotech and genetic engineering are bringing about new species and will lead to the alteration of Homo sapiens. Nanotechnology is manipulating the substances we use down to the subatomic level. Communications technologies will soon link everything to everything. And developments in quantum theory place us in ever-expanding infinities of multiple universes, the histories of which we create, thereby altering everything we understand about ourselves and reality itself. How are we to make sense of all of this? Technology changes the world in which we live, but it also changes us by profoundly altering the structures of our consciousness. It is these changes that I am addressing in my current work.

You can find out more at www.johnlobell.com.

Credits

Page 88. Hostels and Lounge Buildings, Sher-E-Bangla-Nagar, Dacca, Bangladesh. Photo by Henry N. Wilcots.

Page 88. Hostels and Lounge Buildings, Sher-E-Bangla-Nagar, Dacca, Bangladesh. Photo by Anwar Hosain.

Page 91. Model of the National Assembly Hall, Sher-E-Bangla-Nagar, Dacca, Bangladesh. Photo by George Pohl.

Page 92. The National Assembly Hall, Sher-E-Bangla-Nagar, Dacca, Bangladesh. Photo by Henry N. Wilcots.

Page 92. Model of the National Assembly Hall, Sher-E-Bangla-Nagar, Dacca, Bangladesh. Photo by George Pohl.

Pages 95-98. Kimbell Art Museum. Photos by Bob Wharton. Courtesy of the Kimbell Art Museum, Fort Worth, Texas.

Pages 101-103. The Library of the Phillips Exeter Academy, Exeter, New Hampshire. Photos by John Lobell.

Page 104. The Library of the Phillips Exeter Academy, Exeter, New Hampshire. Photo by John Nicolais.

Page 107. The Yale Center for British Art and Studies, New Haven, Connecticut. Photo by Thomas A. Brown.

Pages 108-109. The Yale Center for British Art and Studies, New Haven, Connecticut. Photos by John Lohell.

Page 110. Model of the Yale Center for British Art and Studies, New Haven, Connecticut. Photo by George Pohl.

Page 114. Louis I. Kahn. Photo by Joan Ruggles.

ADDITIONAL CREDITS

Page 64. Excerpts from the *Tao Te Ching* by Lao Tsu, translated by Gia-fu-Feng and Jane English, © 1972. Reprinted by special arrangement with Alfred A. Knopf, Inc.

Page 70. Excerpts from "The Hollow Men," in *Collected Poems 1909-1962* by T. S. Eliot, © 1967. Reprinted by special arrangement with Harcourt Brace Jovanovich, Inc., and Faber and Faber, Ltd.

Pages 86 and 90. Excerpts from "Remarks," by Louis I. Kahn in *Perspecta 9/10: The Yale Architectural Journal,* © 1965. Reprinted by special arrangement with Yale University.

Bibliography

Note: Bracket numbers [ ] in the text refer to the books numbered below.

GENERAL ARCHITECTURE

1. Fletcher, Banister. *A History of Architecture on the Comparative Method.* 18th ed. New York: Scribners, 1975. In the Beaux-Arts tradition in which Louis Kahn was trained, architects poured over and traced plans and elevations from large volumes illustrating historical architecture. Today these great books are found only in rare book collections. Although Banister Fletcher's compact book is not as grand as some of its earlier companions, it is rich in detail.

2. Norwich, John Julius, ed. *Great Architecture of the World.* New York: Random House, American Heritage, 1975. There are many illustrated books available on world architecture; this one is particularly clear and useful.

MODERN ARCHITECTURE

3. Jeanneret, Charles (Le Corbusier). *Towards a New Architecture.* New York: Praeger, 1946.

4. Kaufmann, Edgar, and Ben Raeburn, eds. *Frank Lloyd Wright: Writings and Buildings.* New York: New American Library, Meridian Books, 1960.

5. Scully, Vincent Jr. *Frank Lloyd Wright.* New York: Braziller, 1960.

6. Scully, Vincent Jr. *Modern Architecture.* Rev. ed. New York: Braziller, 1974.

7. Wright, Frank Lloyd. *The Future of Architecture.* New York: Horizon, 1953.

8. Wright, Frank Lloyd. "The Language of Organic Architecture." In *Architectural Forum* (May, 1953).

GENERAL BOOKS ON LOUIS KAHN

9. Chang, Ching-Yu, ed. "Louis I. Kahn: Memorial Issue." *Architecture and Urbanism.* Tokyo: A & U Publishing Co., Ltd., 1975.

10. Giurgola, Romaldo, and Jaimini Mehta. *Louis I. Kahn.* Boulder, Colorado: Westview Press, 1975. Giurgola's and Mehta's book is a thorough interpretation of Kahn's philosophy in the context of modern Western thought. It also relates Kahn's philosophy to his architecture. There are plans and black and white photo-graphs of Kahn's important buildings. Kahn collaborated on the writing of this book.

11. Ronner, Heinz, Sharad Jhaveri, and Alessandro Vasella, eds. *Louis I. Kahn: Complete Works, 1935-74.* Boulder, Colorado: Westview Press, 1977. As indicated by the title, this book contains Kahn's complete works. The book is large and expensive, but is an invaluable source of Kahn's seldom published work. It also includes the early sketches and designs for most of his projects. A complete list of all of Kahn's buildings, and a complete bibliography of writings on Kahn are included.

OTHER WORKS ON LOUIS KAHN
(Some of these are of specialized interest.)

12. Chang, Ching-Yu, ed. "Louis I. Kahn: Silence and Light." *Architecture and Urbanism,* vol. 3, no. 1 (Tokyo, 1973).

13. "Clearing," (Interviews with Louis I. Kahn). In *VIA 2, Structures Implicit and Explicit,* edited by James Bryan and Rolf Sauer. The Student Publication of the Graduate School of Fine Arts. Philadelphia, Pennsylvania: University of Pennsylvania, 1973.

14. Johnson, Nell E., ed. *Light is the Theme: Louis I. Kahn and the Kimbell Art Museum.* Fort Worth, Texas: Kimbell Art Foundation, 1975.

15. Jordy, William H. *American Buildings and Their Architects: The Impact of European Modernism in the Mid-Twentieth Century,* vol. 4. New York: Doubleday, Anchor Books, 1976. Jordy's book has an excellent chapter on Kahn's Richards Medical Research Building.

16. Kahn, Louis I. "Remarks." *Perspecta,* edited by Robert A. M. Stern, vol. 9/10. New Haven, Connecticut: The Yale Architectural Journal, 1965.

17. Kahn, Louis I. "Silence." In *VIA 1, Ecology in Design.* University of Pennsylvania, Philadelphia, Pennsylvania: The Student Publication of the Graduate School of Fine Arts, 1968.

18. Kahn, Louis I. Unpublished transcript of a lecture at Pratt Institute. Brooklyn, New York: 1973.

19. Kahn, Louis I. Unpublished transcripts of various talks and conversations.

20. Komendant, A. L. *18 Years with Architect Louis I. Kahn.* Englewood, New Jersey: Alvray, 1975. Komendant was the engineer for several of Kahn's buildings, and he describes in detail how they were built.

21. Leperé, Yves, Pierre Lacombe, and Renée Diamant-Berger.

L'Architecture d'Aujourd'hui (Issue on Louis I. Kahn), no. 142 (Boulogne: France. Feb/March, 1969).

22. Lobell, John. "Kahn and Venturi; An Architecture of Being-in-Context." *Artforum,* vol. XVI, no. 6 (February, 1978).

23. McLaughlin, Patricia. "How'm I Doing, Corbusier?" (Interview of Louis Kahn). Philadelphia, Pennsylvania: *Pennsylvania Gazette,* vol. 71, no. 3 (December, 1972).

24. Mohlor, Ann, ed. "Louis I. Kahn: Talks with Students." In *Architecture at Rice 26.* Texas: Rice University, 1969.

25. Namuth, Hans and Paul Falkenberg, (producers & directors) *Louis I. Kahn: Architect.* A film. New York: Distributed by Museum at Large Ltd.

26. Pennsylvania Academy of the Fine Arts. *The Travel Sketches of Louis I. Kahn.* A catalogue for an exhibition. Philadelphia, Pennsylvania: Pennsylvania Academy of the Fine Arts, 1978-1979. Introduction by Vincent Scully.

27. Prown, Jules David. *The Architecture of the Yale Center for British Art.* New Haven, Connecticut: Yale University Press, 1977. The story of the construction of the Center illustrated with plans, sketches, and photographs.

28. Scully, Vincent Jr. *Louis I. Kahn.* New York: Braziller, 1962. An excellent analysis of Kahn's work up to 1962. This book is now out-of-print.

29. Unpublished transcripts of memorials for Louis Kahn. Held in Philadelphia and New York in 1974.

30. Wurman, R. S. and E. Feldman, eds. *The Notebooks and Drawings of Louis I. Kahn.* Cambridge, Mass.: MIT Press, 1972.

OTHER BOOKS REFERRED TO

31. Bronowski, J. *The Identity of Man.* Rev. ed. Garden City, New York: Natural History Press, 1971.

32. Eliot, T. S. "The Hollow Men." *T. S. Eliot Selected Poems.* New York: Harcourt Brace Jovanovich, Harbrace Paperbound Library, 1967.

33. Grene, Marjorie. "Heidegger, Martin." In *The Encyclopedia of Philosophy.* New York: Macmillan Publishing Co., The Free Press, 1967.

34. Lao Tzu. *Tao Te Ching.* Translated by Gia-Fu-Feng and Jane English. New York: Alfred A. Knopf, 1972. This translation is the source for the quotes from Lao Tzu used in this book. Lao Tzu's name has several different spellings.

35. Spengler, Oswald. *The Decline of the West.* New York: Alfred A. Knopf, 1939. (Also available in an abridged edition from: New York: Random House, Modern Library, 1965.) Spengler's book interprets history in terms of the world's great cultures and their inner symbolic meaning. This approach gives him a valuable insight into architecture.

ADDITIONAL RESOURCES OF INTEREST

Brownlee, David Bruce, with David G. De Long. *Louis I. Kahn: In the Realm of Architecture.* New York: Rizzoli International Publications, 1991. This is the catalog for a major Kahn exhibition, and is very comprehensive. (There is also a condensed edition).

Giurgola, Romaldo. *Louis I. Kahn.* Zurich: Artemis, 1979. Includes Giurgola's discussions, formulated with Kahn, of the philosophical basis of Kahn's work. Although abstract, this is one of the most profound discussions of Kahn and of architecture we have.

Goldhagen, Sarah Williams. *Louis Kahn's Situated Modernism.* New Haven: Yale University Press, 2001. Goldhagen presents the progressive social intentions of modern architecture immediately after World War II and Kahn's place in that context. But Kahn's work when he had this approach was undistinguished. It was not until he began to see architecture in a deeply artistic, cultural, and spiritual context that Kahn began to design his great buildings. Goldhagen does not address this aspect of Kahn's career.

Kahn, Nathaniel, writer and director. *My Architect: A Son's Journey.* Louis Kahn Project, Inc., 2003. A film exploring Kahn's life and buildings. By interweaving his search for his father with Kahn's biography, Nathaniel Kahn presents a rich portrait of Louis Kahn. Striking footage of Kahn's buildings; archival footage of Kahn speaking; and interviews with Kahn's family, those with whom he had relationships, and colleagues are all brought together to present Kahn and his work with great depth.

Leslie, Thomas. *Louis I. Kahn: Building Art, Building Science.* New York: George Braziller, 2005. Insight into how Kahn's buildings are put together.

McCarter, Robert. *Louis I Kahn.* London and New York: Phaidon Press, 2005. The definitive work on Kahn's architecture. More than five hundred pages addressing Kahn's life; his work in the context of what was happening contemporaneously in architecture; and Kahn's relationship to other architects, particularly Frank Lloyd Wright. Each of Kahn's projects is presented in detail, including early schemes. The book is rich with photographs, plans, drawings, and selections of Kahn's writing, and it includes a chronology and a bibliography.

Larson, Kent. *Louis I. Kahn: Unbuilt Masterworks.* New York: Monacelli, 2000. Computer generated color images of Kahn's key unbuilt buildings. Larson also presents a thoughtful analysis of the role of light in architecture and in Kahn's work.

Rykwert, Joseph, and Roberto Schezen. *Louis Kahn.* New York: Harry N. Abrams, 2001. Magnificent photographs of Kahn's key buildings.

Twombly, Robert, ed. *Louis Kahn: Essential Texts.* New York: W. W. Norton & Company, 2003. Selection of Kahn's writing. (For the most part Kahn's "writings" are transcriptions of his talks and interviews.) Included is his 1973 talk at Pratt Institute, which is a primary source for *Between Silence and Light.*